A

THE **STRUGGLE** FOR THE
Holy Land

© 2015 - Omer Salem / Averroës Books
All rights reserved.

No part of this book may be used or reproduced by any means, graphic, electronic, or mechanical, including photocopying, recording, taping or by any information storage retrieval system without the written permission of the author /publisher except in the case of brief quotations embodied in critical articles and reviews.

Contat Professor Salem at **omer.salem@aya.yale.edu**

Averroës Books is an imprint of the **Ibn Rushd Institute**
ibnrushd.org

ISBN: 978-0-9864494-9-9 - *softcover*
978-0-9864494-7-5 - *hardcover*
978-0-9864494-8-2 - *e-book*

PUBLISHED IN THE UNITED STATES OF AMERICA

BOOK DESIGN
www.timmyroland.com

COVER IMAGE
www.shutterstock.com

بسم الله الرحمن الرحيم

THE **STRUGGLE** FOR THE HOLY LAND

"O mankind! We created you from a single (pair) of a male and a female, and made you into nations and tribes, that ye may know each other. Verily the most honored of you in the sight of Allah is the person who is the most virtuous of you."

Qur'an 49:13

THE **STRUGGLE** FOR THE HOLY LAND

Endorsements

"Very thoughtful and thought-provoking, and you have presented a different way of regarding the Arab-Israeli conflict from a moral and human point of view. I liked in particular your proposal for inviting the Arab Jews back to their homes in the Arab world. I'm sure this is an excellent way forward and defeats the hostility that Israel has created towards the Arabs."

        Ghada Karmi, Palestinian Native of Jerusalem
        Professor of Arab and Islamic Studies, Exeter University, Devon, UK

"I found this thoughtful, moving, learned, and persuasive. Thank you for sharing it with me, and I wish you all the best in getting this message out. It would be wonderful to hear a million voices urging precisely what you put forth!"

        Jeremy F. Hultin, Professor of New Testament
        Yale Divinity School, Yale University, New Haven, Connecticut, USA

"I just want to bless you for your warm heart that seeks to build a bridge between Arabs and Jews. I encourage you to keep up your efforts."

        Bishop Brian Cox, Episcopal Priest
        International Center for Religion and Diplomacy
        Washington, District of Columbia, USA

"Incredible and has made me think in new ways. I am very grateful to you for sharing this with me."

Rabbi Ephraim Gabbai
Sixteenth Street Synagogue, New York City, New York, USA

"I am profoundly grateful for your most helpful and insightful work. Thank you for your lifetime of scholarship that has led to your ability to write such a significant contribution to the challenges you address. I wonder, would you allow me to send your paper or a link to your paper to three colleagues? I'm sure they would be very interested as they share your concerns and would appreciate your scholarship and helpful insights. May God keep blessing and guiding you and your work."

Gordon Scruton
Bishop of the Episcopal Church, Springfield, Massachusetts, USA

"You have done a lot of work, and carefully thought through the great tangle of problems which present themselves to any potential peaceful resolution of the problems faced in the Middle East . . . I think the basic principles that you are espousing are the correct principles that we will have to follow if we are to make progress on these very difficult matters . . . I am glad that you are doing what you are doing."

Dick Jacobsen, Stake President of LDS Church
Redwood City, California, USA

"Omer, thank you for the paper, it is very inspiring."

Rabbi Patricia Karlin-Neumann
Senior Associate Dean for Religious Life
Stanford University, Palo Alto, California, USA

"I think this is probably the best work you have done so far. You are mastering the method we think will work best: using the orthodox religious text to support the belief that God wants all humans to speak their truth honestly and at the same time to be patient with each other's conflicting religious beliefs - not forcing agreement today, but letting God make things clear at the Final Hour" Q5:48

Charles Randal Paul Founder and President
Foundation for Religious Diplomacy New York, New York, USA

"I just finished reading your paper - amazing! Thanks so much for sending it again. I really appreciate the Qur'anic verses supporting your solutions, and remembering the positive heritage of Islam, for instance, the Muslims sheltering the Spanish Jews."

Vicky Sigworth, Yale Faculty Spouse
Youth For Christ Organization, New Haven, Connecticut, USA

"Thanks for your paper. I enjoyed reading it . . . you certainly raise a number of issues that I have not heard before. Your comments make me hopeful because: You bring an understanding of Arab history that's not generally known in the West. You propose specific actions that Arab governments can implement that would benefit Jews without jeopardizing Arab security [and] You emphasize the importance of a religious solution in the Middle East, a topic that is often minimized by Western diplomacy . . . It is very interesting to me that you are interested enough in this topic to spend several years learning more about the languages of the Bible."

Kenneth Godshall
Master in Divinity, Yale Divinity School
Yale University, New Haven, Connecticut, USA

"I found the thesis fascinating and I must say, I was moved by the proposal of inviting Jews to live in Arab lands."

Mohammad Khalil
Professor of Middle Eastern Studies
Michigan State University, Lansing, Michigan, USA

"I thoroughly enjoyed reading it and am very encouraged and moved by your ideas. ... I think for the Christian community many people would be very surprised - and pleased - that a Muslim would approach the issue in such a way. The idea of Q41:34 equating to loving enemies is not one that I have ever heard propounded - either by Muslims or Christian interpreters of Islam...certainly to break the deadlock someone has to take the first step and in a sense be willing to risk suffering injustice."

Philip McCollum Department of Sociology
School of Humanities and Social Sciences
Exeter University, Devon, UK

"I found your insight on the conflict being not so much about the land, but connected to the land to be a significant one. Bringing this to the attention of all involved will be helpful. As to your comments on my own religious community in terms of evangelical Christians, you have correctly noted the significance of views related to blessings and curses related to those who help Israel. Perhaps even more important is your recognition of dispensationalist views of biblical prophecy to how Israel and "Palestine" are viewed. This is perhaps the most significant factor as many popular "End Times" views place Israel as significant with various characters playing the "anti-Christ."

John W. Morehead
Evangelical Christian Foundation for Religious Diplomacy
New York City, New York, USA

"Throughout your nice analysis of your [six] points, I was struck with this nagging feeling that Muslims, especially Arabs, now and in the past, have been, and still are, responsible and thus accountable for the pathetic situation of Jewish and non-Jewish people of the Holy Land... It is, indeed, commendable and necessary to remind ourselves and everyone else to be compassionate and merciful, as has been ordered by Allah (SWT)."

Ali Shakibai, MD
Tehran University of Medical Sciences, Faculty of Medicine,
Tehran, Iran

"Indeed, [the paper] does represent a unique and engaging position on the middle-east peace process."

Peter Salovey, Provost
Yale University, New Haven, Connecticut, USA

"I just finished reading the paper. It is EXCELLENT. If Jews, Christians and Muslims lived their religion and gave others the same right and respect the world would be at peace. The problem is people not the Holy Bible, the Torah or the Qur'an."

Boyd Smith, Stake President
The Church of Jesus Christ for Later Day Saints
Palo Alto, California, USA

"It is an excellently written paper. I am excited that it places, what I feel, proper emphasis on the role of religion in the region. The appeal to Islamic Moral Values is a very powerful argument."

Benjamin Abrahamson
Orthodox Hasidic Jew, Judge in Israeli Religious Courts
Mea Shearim, Jerusalem, State of Israel

THE **STRUGGLE** FOR THE HOLY LAND

CONTENTS

Definition of Terms	i
Introduction	v
Arab Awakening: Holy Bible and Holy Qur'an	1
The World is more Religious	5
The Jews and the Land	8
One Patriarch many Denominations	12
Commonalities and Differences	14
The First Point: the Oppressed in the Land	17
Radical Islam and the Conflict	21
Replace PLO with HLCO	25
The Second Point: the Scattered in the Land	27
Brief History of the Jews	31
The Nature of the Conflict	34
Jews in Arab Land	36
Objections to Repatriation	43
Jews and Arab Enmity	44
Dignitism as Path to Peace	47
Jews as Neighbors	49
Only seek Allah	51
The Return of Refugees	53
Who May Finance Repatriation	56
Zionists do not want Peace	57
Zionist Aggression Rewarded	60
Zionists may Refuse Repatriation	61
Zionists and their Ploy	62
Arabs are Cheated Again	64
The Third Point: The Holy Land	65

Palestine or Holy Land	67
Jerusalem and Mecca	70
Each Revelation is Unique	72
The Fourth Point: The Purpose of Scripture	74
The Purpose of the Qur'an	76
Ways to Reduce the Conflict	79
The Fifth Point: Virtue of Mercy and Learning	82
The Holy Quran and the Holy Tanakh	85
Religion and Government	87
The Sixth Point: Dignitism and Peace	89
Tolerance and Respect	92
The Keys of the Holy Sepulcher	97
Abrahamic Traditions Are Helpful Rivals	99
Conclusion	102
Summary points to solve conflict	104
Epilogue	109
Exhibit One	113
Exhibit Two	119
Exhibit Three	122
Bibliography	123
About the Author	127

THE **STRUGGLE** FOR THE
Holy Land

Omer **Salem**

NEW HAVEN, CONNECTICUT

THE **STRUGGLE** FOR THE HOLY LAND

Definition of Terms

Arab: A member of a Semitic people inhabiting much of the Middle East and North Africa.

Ahlul Kitab: people of the book as defined in the Holy Qur'an chapter Anaam (6:156). this term usually refers to Jews and Christians.

Ahlul Qur'an: people of the Quran, which refers to the followers of prophet Muhammad, the Muslim people.

Bantustan: an area designated for Palestinian people in the Holy Land. The term is used to designate that areas A and B in the West Bank per the Oslo Accords have become apartheid ghettos akin to the real Bantustans of the apartheid era south Africa.

Dhimmi (Arabic: ذمي) the name applied by the Muslim conquerors to indigenous non-Muslim populations who surrendered by a treaty (dhimma) to Muslim domination.

Dignitism is the state of living one's religious ideals while honoring those who strive to live their religious ideals. Religious ideal means peace with God, self and neighbor. In Arabic we call that Ihsan. Ihsan is treating others with respect, integrity and kindness.

Hasidic Jew: branch of Judaism that promotes spirituality and joy through the popularization and internalization of Jewish mysticism.

Ihsan (Arabic: إحسان), is an Arabic term meaning "perfection" or "excellence" . It is a matter of taking one's inner faith (iman) and showing it in both deed and action, a sense of social responsibility borne from religious convictions.

Islam: The religion of the Muslims, a monotheistic faith regarded as revealed through Muhammad as the Prophet of Allah.

Islam: The religion of the people before the prophet Muhammad and after him, who submit to one God, a monotheistic faith regarded as revealed through the prophet Ibrahim and all his decedents.

Israeli: a native or national of the State of Israel, a person of Israeli decent.

Jizya (Arabic: جزية) is the money, or tribute, "that conquered non-Muslims historically had to pay to their Islamic overlords 'with willing submission and while feeling themselves subdued' to safeguard their existence.

Kabbalah: The ancient Jewish tradition of mystical interpretation of the Bible, first transmitted orally and using esoteric methods

MENA: The term MENA, for "Middle East and North Africa", is an acronym often used in academic and business writing.

Muslim: A follower of the religion of Islam, found by the Patriarch Abraham and restored by the Prophet Muhammad.

Muslim Brotherhood: An Islamic religious and political organization dedicated to the establishment of a nation based on Islamic principles.

Orthodox Jew: A Jew who practices strict observance of Mosaic law.

Palestinian: A member of the native Arab population of the region of Palestine- including the State of Israel founded in 1948.

Pious Jew: a Jew who promotes spirituality and joy through the popularization and internalization of Jewish mysticism as the fundamental aspects of the Jewish faith. This term could apply to Jews of all denominations whether internalizing mysticism or not; and many who reject mysticism could still be pious.

Salafi: a Muslim who emphasizes the Salaf ("predecessors"), the earliest Muslims, as model examples of Islamic practice.

Israeli Settlers: members of civilian Jewish communities in the West Bank.

Sufi: A Muslim ascetic and mystic

Tablighi: member of Tablighi Ja جماعة التبليغ English: Society for spreading faith) is a transnational Muslim religious movement.

Ummah (Arabic: أمة) is an Arabic word meaning "nation" or "community". It is distinguished from Sha'b (Arabic: شعب) which means a nation with common ancestry or geography.

Wahhabi: a member of a strictly orthodox Sunni Muslim sect from Saudi Arabia; strives to purify Islamic beliefs and rejects any innovations.

Zionist: relating to or characteristic of Zionism; "the Zionist movement". A Jewish movement for (originally) the reestablishment and (now) the development and protection of a Jewish nation in Israel.

THE **STRUGGLE** FOR THE HOLY LAND

INTRODUCTION

Religion plays an important role in the lives and daily practices of most people in the Middle East[1]. Ninety nine percent of the inhabitants of the Middle East self identify as part of the Abrahamic faith. The remaining 1% could be atheists or members of other religions. The 99% trace their common origin to the Patriarch Abraham (d. 1650 BCE). About 2% of the inhabitants of the Middle East trace the origin of their faith to the Prophet Abraham through his son Isaac—they call their faith and that of Abraham Judaism. Another 6% of the inhabitants of the Middle East trace their faith to the Prophet Abraham through his son Isaac—they call their faith and that of Abraham Christianity.

The majority of the inhabitants of the Middle East, about 92%, self-identify and trace the origin of their faith to the Prophet Abraham through his son Ishmael—they call their faith and that of Abraham—Islam. The Holy Qur'an defines Islam as the name of the restored religion of the Patriarch Abraham. However, today, Islam is widely known as the religion of the followers of the Prophet Muhammad. Muslims regard Abraham as a prophet and patriarch, the archetype of the perfect Muslim, and the revered reformer of the Kaaba in Mecca. While 92% of Arabs are Muslims, only 18% of Muslims are Arabs. The Arab Awakening of 2011 used the moral values of religion as a unifying and driving force to get rid of despotic regimes and their corruption. As outer form of religiosity, crowds in Tahrir Square, and elsewhere, expressed their religiosity by kneeling and prostrating themselves while security forces attacked them.

Just as Islamic moral values were used as basis for the Arab Awakening and uprisings, this paper argues that Islamic moral values could also establish peace and justice for both the Holy Land Arabs and the Holy Land Jews in the Arab-Israeli conflict. For Arabs in the Middle East, the Islamic tradition and the Holy Qur'an should be the predominant source of peacemaking efforts; any attempts to use or rely on the UN charter, international law, the constitution of the various Arab states or any other text or document to propose peace will likely fail because Arabs who claim Islam as their religion and live in the Middle East have little respect for any document or text as compared to the respect they have for the Holy Qur'an. This should not be surprising to Western scholars and it should be taken as an opportunity to hold the Arabs to the Islamic moral values taught in their own books as basis to normalize relations with the Jewish State.

This paper will offer ample evidence in the Holy Qur'an and Hadith that is consistent with the teachings in the Bible. One could use Islamic moral values in conflict resolution such as: guarding the tongue, prohibition on gossip, bigotry and prejudice. Appointing credible and God-fearing judges recognizable by both sides is the key to achieving inter-religious peace in the Holy Land. The main argument in this paper is focused on the primary objections, on religious and non-religious grounds, to peace with the Jewish State. The paper addresses those objections using the Holy Qur'an and the Hadith tradition. In this paper God and Allah are used interchangeably. Arab-ring governments refer primarily to Egypt, Kingdom of Saudi Arabia ("KSA"), Syria, Lebanon, Jordan, Palestinian Authority and Iraq. Arab governments refer to all 22 countries members of the Arab League. The paper proposes a workable two state solution.

We have an ancient biblical story being played in Palestine, the Land of Israel, and the Holy Land mentioned in the Bible. There are multiple biblical claims to these lands. Each group claims to be the people described in the Bible, The Hebrews clearly have a distinction from the writings of the Bible and Qur'an. Arabs have lived in these lands as long as the Hebrews and also have a claim to the land. The Philistines are mentioned by name in the Hebrew Bible and by reference in the Qur'an. However, God bequeathed the Holy Land to the Children of Abraham in the Bible and Qur'an in eternal covenant. Both, the Arabs and the Hebrews view themselves as the legitimate heirs to the prophet or the patriarch Abraham.

In the author's view, the struggle is not between the Bible and the Qur'an, for both scriptures complement each other. The struggle is between those who claim to interpret the Bible and Qur'an. We will see herein the inherent harmony between our scriptures and consequent hope for reconciliation.

Semantics can be a stumbling block, so I would like to clarify the terms often used and then move ahead to better terminology—terminology that will speak to both sides. The Bible refers to the Holy Land with the following terms: the land of Canaan, the land of the Philistines, the Land of Israel, and the Holy Land. Each of these terms is loaded with meaning. The Qur'an uses the term Holy Land, the Blessed Land, the Land of Aqsa Mosque—here we see that both books agree on the term "Holy Land", and is the term I personally favor.

Biblical and Qur'anic sources are remarkably similar regarding the relationship of the Jewish people to the Holy Land. The Bible mentions the Holy Land in the book of Exodus (3:5) and the Qur'an shows reverence for the Holy Land in the chapter of al-Ma'idah (5:21). What goes wrong is when these quotes are taken out of context for political ends. Herein I will familiarize you with our scriptural sources, discuss how these sources were mistakenly used, and how we can understand our scriptures to bring lasting peace between our peoples.

First, where does the term "Palestine" come from? The land of the Philistines ("Palestine") is a term mentioned in many places in the Hebrew Bible including the book of Genesis (21:34): "And Abraham stayed in the land of the Philistines for a long time." The Philistines saw the establishment of the kingdom of Israel (1030 to 960 BCE). When the Romans destroyed the second Temple in 70 CE, bringing an end to the second Jewish commonwealth, the Romans renamed the Holy Land "Palestine", in part to insult the Jews who had warred with the Philistines. This term then became the common term to refer to this land.

Second, while the term Israel is first mentioned in the book of Genesis, the term "Land of Israel" is first mentioned in First Samuel 13:19: "Not a blacksmith could be found in the whole land of Israel, because the Philistines had said, "Otherwise the Hebrews will make swords or spears!" Jews feel that they have returned to the land of Israel which was promised to them by God. In 1948, the state of Israel was restored (according to the Jewish people) and taken by force (according to the Arab people) in Palestine.

In my opinion, the Palestinian Arabs are struggling to defend what they refer to as the Land of the Philistines - a term which existed more than three millenniums ago, referring to a people who no longer exist. At the same time, the Jews are struggling to have peace with their neighbors after returning to what they call the Land of Israel. Both sides think they have achieved some gains in their struggle over the land, but in fact those gains are only imaginary. Why? Because the Jews failed to find a peace partner or live in peace in the Land of Israel, while the Palestinians failed to have a viable state they can call home and live with dignity in the Land of Palestine. Each side blames the other side for their failure.

I herein propose that the parties have not addressed essential issues in striving for peace. Peace has to be grounded in their respective holy books. While the name Palestine is distasteful to many Jews because of historical enmity, the name Israel is not appreciated by many Arabs because of modern enmity. Thus I suggest the utilization of the term "Holy Land", grounded in both the Bible and Qur'an, to help bring both parties closer to an agreement.

---

1 - In this paper the Middle East is defined to consist of the following countries (Egypt, Israel, Iran, Iraq, Jordan, Lebanon, Palestine, KSA, Syria, Turkey) The Future of the Global Muslim Population. Pew Research Center Retrieved 22 December 2011.

THE **STRUGGLE** FOR THE
Holy Land

Omer **Salem**

THE **STRUGGLE** FOR THE HOLY LAND

Arab Awakening
THE HOLY QUR'AN AND THE BIBLE

The Arab Awakening of 2011 took everyone, including Arabs, by surprise. From Western governments to now-deposed leaders in the Middle East, it was unexpected. All four countries that had regime changes (Egypt, Libya, Tunisia and Yemen) shared four factors: aging autocratic rulers, high levels of corruption and nepotism, lack of dignity for ordinary citizens, and police brutality. Because these failed regimes were endorsed, supported and on-occasions praised, by various American administrations, USA reputation in the Middle East stands to suffer for some time to come. For America to be viewed, by Arabs and Muslims, as the endorsers of corrupt dictatorial regimes speaks volume about how America spends its resources and its political capital. As the American President Barak Obama declared in his 2009 historic speech in Cairo:

> *"All people yearn for certain things: the ability to speak your mind and have a say in how you are governed; confidence in the rule of law and the equal administration of justice; government that is transparent and does not steal from the people and the freedom to live as you choose."*[1]

Revolutionists in the recent Arab Awakening drew on their people's Islamic values and traditions to fuel the uprisings that toppled their regimes. While revolutions relied on technology and mass media, it was the people's reliance on religious moral values as delineated in a book titled: *La Morale Du*

*Coran, The Revolution Succeeded.*² that made the revolutions succeed. This is reflected in the fact that all autocratic regime changes in those countries involves replacing existing regimes by religiously leaning parties, parliaments, and or governments. No one in the West predicted those revolutions, and there is only speculation about where they might go. As the Middle East specialist, the American journalist, author and three times winner of the Pulitzer Prize writes for New York Times, "If you did not see it coming, what makes you think you know where it is going?"³ It is likely, however, that the Arab Awakening will result in yet another conflict with the State of Israel for two primary reasons: Firstly, the State of Israel is viewed as a (pariah state) common enemy among all Arabs; Secondly, most religious leaders in the Arab world hold anti-Zionists views which leads to anti-Jewish and anti-Israel views. They can always find media reports that justify their position. That is why in the Middle East Israel is not viewed as a good neighbor to have, but as a colonial aggressor to uproot, by force if necessary. Therefore, it is important to find a solution for this nagging and untamed conflict, before more innocent blood from both sides is spilled.

For many years, the Arab-Israeli conflict has seemed intractable.⁴ Its solution has eluded most world and regional political leaders on all sides. In the words of a Yale University scholar, this conflict is becoming more and more like the Greek classic legend of Phrygian Gordium the "Gordian Knot."⁵ The legend is associated with Alexander the Great. It is often used as a metaphor for an intractable problem solved by "thinking outside the box". In this paper an "out of the box" solution is discussed and surprisingly, it is simple elegant and supported by wise and educated people on both sides of the conflict. First, the question I would like to propose in this paper is: Why has the Arab-Israeli violent conflict over Palestine lasted for sixty seven years with no end in sight? What can be done to peacefully end the violent conflict between Arabs and Jews over Palestine? Could the recent Arab Awakening help Arabs make peace with Israel? The answer I would like to suggest in this paper is: **the Arab Israeli conflict is intractable because some of the participants and many observers and would-be peace makers have focused primarily on political and economic solutions and have sidelined or marginalized the elephant in the room—religion.** Religion in this context means the religion of Islam and the religion of People of the Book (Jews and Christians). Because the religion of Islam does not separate between church and state, the religion of Islam becomes political Islam. According to Peter Beaumont, the British Journalist and Author of *"The Secret Life of War: Journeys through Modern Conflict"*, The ;Arab Awakening showed in no unequivocal terms that "political Islam is poised to dominate the new world order."[6]

According to John Louis Esposito, a professor of International Affairs and Islamic Studies and the director of the Prince Alwaleed Bin Talal Center for Muslim-Christian Understanding at Georgetown University, "Political Islam is a set of ideologies holding that Islam is as much a political ideology as a religion".[7] Anticipating that Islam would dominate world politics, Professor Harry Attridge, Dean of Yale Divinity School, indicated that relations between Islam and the West "are critical to the fate of the planet."[8] The Arab Israeli conflict is at the heart and center of such relations. President Obama's National Security Advisor, General James Jones, put it more starkly when he said the Palestinian-Israeli conflict is the "epicenter" of many problems. It ripples around the globe and solving it would help the United Sates address other challenges. Therefore, if there were one problem to solve in the world, this would be it.[9]

In other words, a) Arabs and Muslims view this conflict as the basis for many others around the world—Although, someone might argue that the conflict is a convenient way for MENA political leaders to draw attention away from other problems that plague the Muslim and Arab world, such as, slavery in Mauritania, massacres in Algeria, Christians in Egypt and Iraq, Al-Qaeda in Libya, massacres in Syria, the Kafeel system in KSA and WMD aspirations in Iran.[10] b) the conflict is intractable because political leaders do not openly address the religious aspects of the conflict. c) political Islam is poised to dominate, not necessarily because Muslim Jihadi groups like to chop off everyone's head or hand but because, in their view, all other solutions to the conflict have failed. All other solutions mean secular solutions both political and economic. Secular solutions have failed because they have the implicit promise of material gain or material success, a peace dividend, the economic benefit of a decrease in defense spending which account for 6% to 11% of the GDP of MENA countries.[11] Many economic plans were introduced to end the conflict including the annual aid by USA to both Egypt and Israel, yet, economic benefits alone will not solve the conflict - a religious solution must be contemplated.

---

1 - Lisa Anderson, Demystifying the Arab Spring, Foreign Affairs, May 2011. P4
2 - Mohamed Abdullah Daraz, Le Morale Du Coran (Paris: Rissalla, 1951), translated to English under the title: A. M. Daraz, Introduction to the Quran, (London: I.B. Tauris, 2000), and translated to Arabic under the title: A.S. Shahin, The constitution of Morales in the Quran, دستور الاخلاق في القرآن.
3 - Thomas Freedman, "Watching Elephants Fly," *The New York Times*, January 7, 2012.
4 - The conflict became intractable to the extent that, at Yale University, April 17, 2012, Dr. Abdel Dayem Nosair, a senior adviser to Al Azhar University Grand Imam, said in response to a question about how to solve the conflict, "I do not know of a solution to this conflict; if you have a solution let me know."
5 - According to Merriam-Webster: an intricate problem; especially: a problem insoluble in its own terms —often used in the phrase cut the Gordian knot.
6 - Peter Beaumont, "Political Islam poised to dominate the new world bequeathed by Arab spring", Foreign Affairs Magazine, December 3, 2011.
7 - John L. Esposito and John O. Voll, *Islam and Democracy*, (oxford: Oxford University Press, 1996), p 232.
8 - Harold Attridge, Spectrum Magazine, Yale Divinity School, winter 2012, page 28.
9 - General James Jones' speech on October 27, 2009, at the J street conference "this is the epicenter" (vimeo.com/7302509).
10 - The Kafeel system: a restrictive system of holding a foreign employee-passport, banning him or her from traveling within the Kingdom on his or her own and restricting the freedom of transfer of his or her sponsorship.
11 - The World Fact Book, Central Intelligence Agency. Military Expenditure

THE WORLD
IS MORE RELIGIOUS

In his book *The Desecularization of the World,* Peter Burger of Boston University debunks an important assumption: "the assumption that we live in a secularized world is false. The world today . . . is as furiously religious as it ever was."[1] Among Christians, Evangelicals and Pentecostals are the two segments with substantial increase in adherents. Among Jews, Hasidic and Orthodox are the two segments with substantial increase in adherents.[2]

Among Muslims Salafi and Tablighi are the two segments with substantial increase in adherents. The Holy Book of Islam, the Qur'an, is the most studied, most memorized, and the most respected religious book in the world today, far surpassing the public interest in the Holy Bible.[3] Also, the given name "Mohammed" or "Ahmed" are the most common first name for a male in the world.[4] Therefore, because the world is more religious than secular and religion will continue to dominate world politics, especially in the Middle East, religious solutions must be found before addressing political and economic issues in dealing with the conflict. Why? More suicide bombers are far more willing to give up their lives for religious reasons, than they would for political or economic gain. Resolution to the conflict based on religious moral values (Islamic values which have their equivalent in the Bible) means using such values in conflict resolution. Islamic moral values mean relying on a contemporary and unbiased exegesis of the Holy Qur'an and Hadith.

The most potent argument to make to radical Muslim religious leaders (those holding back peace in the Holy Land) is that according to the Qur'an, God is one and religion is one, but, Shari'a (covenant), is different.[5] This is a key distinction to make as even some scholars tend to confuse both terms—religion and covenant. Therefore, it is important to recognize the difference between Deen (basic religion) and Shari'a (covenant). While, all three Abrahamic faiths, Islam, Christianity and Judaism, are viewed to share the same God and the same Deen (religion), they all have different covenants with God (different Shari'a).[6] The Jews call their covenant with God the Halaka Law, the Catholics call it Canon Law and the Muslims call it Shari'a Law. The ideas expressed in this paper, according to Yale University Political Science Professor Andrew March, are "very bold and original"[7] yet, according to Exeter University Arab and Islamic Studies Professor, Ghada Karmi, the ideas are "very thoughtful and thought-provoking"[8] One should consider these ideas, if one hopes to prevent unpleasant events arising in the Middle East and affecting people in the Middle East and beyond. The conflict is primarily over what those three different but related Abrahamic traditions claim as Holy Places in the region (historically called Palestine). According to a Jewish Zionist they view the primary dynamic in the conflict as Arabs and Muslims refusal to acknowledge the legitimacy of the Jewish State and that all of Palestine is an Islamic Waqf (endowment).[9]

Such claims have led to a sense of a "right of possession" and the right to 'envision' the Holy Land. Each of the three Abrahamic faiths teaches their adherents to emulate the character of the Prophet or Messenger that was assigned to them. Emulation, imitation, and drawing parallels are taken seriously when one identifies specific points of correspondence. These "points of correspondence" become so much more alive when they involve scriptural places, peoples and events. Scriptural places mean such things as the place where the prophet lived or the place where the Holy Scripture was revealed. A plan for lasting resolution would, therefore, require recognition and support of the "other" as a believer, not in the final revelation, but a divine revelation nonetheless. Emphasizing the mutual good-will, supported by their respective scriptures and beliefs, empowers all parties to the conflict to focus on a hopeful future and less on past injustices or differing perceptions of history and rights of possession and sovereignty. In order to have peace in the Holy Land one has to start with a vision of what that peace would look like, then find precedence in history—based on scripture—to aid, sustain, maintain and support such vision.

---

1 - Peter L. Burger, *The Desecularization of the World*, (Michigan: Wm. B. Eerdmans Publishing, 1999) p. 2.
2 - Joseph Berger, "Aided by Orthodox, [NY} City's Jewish Population Is Growing Again", New York Time, June 12, 2012.
3 - Darrell G. Young, Focus on Jerusalem, Prophecy Ministry. www.focusonjerusalem.com.
4 - Muhammad, prophet of Islam. The Columbia Encyclopedia, Sixth Edition. 2001-07
5 - إنَّ الدِّينَ عِندَ اللَّهِ الْإِسْلَامُ The Religion before Allah is Islam (submission to God's Will)" Q3:19
6 - لِكُلٍّ جَعَلْنَا مِنكُمْ شِرْعَةً وَمِنْهَاجًا To each among you have we prescribed a covenant and an open way." Q5:48
7 - Andrew March, Associate Professor, Department of Political Science, Yale University, January 8, 2012, Via email.
8 - Ghada Karmi,, a Palestinian from Jerusalem, Professor of Arab and Islamic Studies, Exter University, Exeter, Devon UK, March 8, 2012, via email.
9 - David Meir-Levi, Zionist Lecturer at San Jose University, via email dated June 13, 2012

THE JEWS
AND THE LAND

In the Jewish tradition, which holds the Torah as the Word of God, "possession" means that the Laws of Torah are administered in one's own life and synagogue. This is why the Children of Israel have operated as a vassal state—in Diaspora—for a lot more years than they ever operated as a completely sovereign state. As long as the requirements of the Torah were met, it was "sufficient" sovereignty[1]. However, in order to fully and freely practice their faith, Jews needed to have a country. They needed to have a place where they are not oppressed or subjugated by other peoples or nations. The concept of "sufficient sovereignty" became insufficient sovereignty, when power politics intervened. In 1917, as the Ottoman Empire—ruler of the Holy Land—was nearing its demise, Arthur Balfour, the Foreign Secretary of Great Britain issued what is commonly cited as Balfour Declaration:

> "His Majesty's government view with favor the establishment in Palestine of a national home for the Jewish people, and will use their best endeavors to facilitate the achievement of this object, it being clearly understood that nothing shall be done which may prejudice the civil and religious rights of existing non-Jewish communities in Palestine, or the rights and political status enjoyed by Jews in any other country."[2]

In a rational world this declaration would have been a win-win for both Jews and Arabs. For, this declaration envisions and promotes safety and security for the Jews while assuring civil and religious rights for the Palestinians. However, in 1939, on the heel of WW2 and for political reasons, Great Britain retracted on its promise:

> *"A policy paper issued by the British government under Neville Chamberlain in which the idea of partitioning the Mandate for Palestine . . . was abandoned in favor of creating an independent Palestine governed by Palestinian Arabs and Jews in proportion to their numbers in the population"* [3]

From the Balfour Declaration to the Chamberlain Declaration, one could clearly see the role of power politics in the granting part of historical Palestine to the Jews and then withdrawing such grant.

According to the Islamic faith, the concept of sovereignty is universal, that is non-territorial, transcendental, meaning beyond human agency, indivisible, inalienable and truly absolute. God, the sovereign, is the primary lawgiver while agents such as the Islamic state and the Khalifa enjoy marginal autonomy necessary to implement and enforce the laws of their sovereign.[4] One could deduct from the above discussion that both the Torah and the Qur'an define and delineate possession and sovereignty in terms that have nothing to do with land ownership, land possession or land control. Both the Holy Torah and the Holy Qur'an say that land belongs to God—not to nations, principalities, kingdoms or states.[5,6]

In a secular world, where considerations on what the Bible or the Qur'an say are secondary, a concept such as land for peace is workable. However, in the Middle East, we no longer live in a secular world. That is why negotiations centered on land for peace, are no longer effective. Such negotiations only serve to embolden extremists on both sides. For example: Zionist extremists say, "look how small the area of the State of

Israel is, we did not occupy any ones land, we were granted land by a recognized world body—the UN. We should not give up land to any one, and we will settle the land—from the river to the sea—by force if necessary".[7] Also, a Zionist Jew may add, Israel has been willing to give up land, and has given up land, and has offered to give up more land; and every Israeli government from Ben Gurion to Netanyahu has pleaded for peaceful resolution and has resorted to force only after lethal provocation.[8]

For which a nationalist Arab will say "the Zionists have no regard now or since 1948, for the inhabitants of Palestine. The Zionists come to colonize and occupy all of Palestine by force and rename it Israel; and now they are negotiating to give us a small piece back so they can keep the rest of our land. We will not allow that to happen, we want all our land back—from the river to the sea—through peaceful negotiations we will get our land back or by force we will get our land back." One would deduct from the above discussion that both the Torah and the Qur'an define and delineate possession and sovereignty in terms that have nothing to do with land ownership, land possession or land control. Both the Holy Torah and the Holy Qur'an say that land belongs to God—not to nations, principalities, kingdoms or states. In the Holy Qur'an Allah said that land belongs to Allah.[9] In the Holy Torah Allah said that land belongs to Allah.[10]

1 - Benjamin Abrahamson, Religious Court Judge in Jerusalem, Israel, via email dated May 15, 2012.
2 - Yapp, M.E. (1987-09-01). *The Making of the Modern Near East 1792-1923.* Harlow, England: Longman. p. 290.
3 - Manchester Guardian 24/5/39 pg.10
4 - M.A. Moqtader Khan, "Sovereignty in Islam as Human Agency"
5 - Deuteronomy 10:14" הֵן לַיהוָה אֱלֹהֶיךָ הַשָּׁמַיִם וּשְׁמֵי הַשָּׁמָיִם הָאָרֶץ וְכָל־אֲשֶׁר־בָּהּ
"Behold, to the LORD your God belong heaven and the heaven of heavens, the Land with all that is in it.
6 - Q7:128 إِنَّ الْأَرْضَ لِلَّهِ يُورِثُهَا مَن يَشَاءُ مِنْ عِبَادِهِ وَالْعَاقِبَةُ لِلْمُتَّقِينَ for the Land is Allah's, to give as a heritage to such of His servants as He pleaseth; and the end is (best) for the righteous."
7 - Baylis Thomas, The Dark Side of Zionism: Israel's Quest for Security Through Dominance (Maryland: Lexington Books, 2009) p45
8 - David Meir-Levi, Zionist Jew Lecturer at San Jose University, via email dated June 13, 2012.Vol 1, No:10 (Dec 30, 1999)
9 - Q7: 128. إِنَّ الْأَرْضَ لِلَّهِ يُورِثُهَا مَن يَشَاءُ مِنْ عِبَادِهِ وَالْعَاقِبَةُ لِلْمُتَّقِينَ.
10 - Deuteronomy 10:14. הֵן לַיהוָה אֱלֹהֶיךָ הַשָּׁמַיִם וּשְׁמֵי הַשָּׁמָיִם הָאָרֶץ וְכָל־אֲשֶׁר־בָּהּ
To the LORD your God belong the heavens, even the highest heavens, the earth and everything in it.

One Patriarch
AND MANY DENOMINATIONS

The Middle East is roughly 92% Muslim and 8% non-Muslim.[1] Any hope of peace and reconciliation in the Middle East has to come from and be based on the religion of the majority of the people there—Islam. For the past decades US and Arab politicians have been trying (or pretending) to find a workable solution—to no avail. From the days of George Marshall in the Truman Administration in the 50's, to the days of George Shultz in the Reagan Administration in the 80's to the recent days of George Mitchell in the current Obama Administration—all political solutions have failed. The latest peace attempt lead by Special Mideast envoy George Mitchell failed because, in the words of Tawfik Hamid of the Jerusalem Post, "Solving the Arab-Israeli conflict must be done initially at the theological level rather than the political level, as the former is impeding the latter"[2].

Daniel Levy, a veteran Israeli peace negotiator who is now at the New America Foundation said of George Mitchell " he hit a brick wall".[3] The brick wall of failed politics could be breached, if and when religious issues are discussed with openness and sincerity. To affect a lasting peaceful solution to the conflict, two important factors must be considered. The first factor is that the solution must be grounded in the religion of the majority of the people there—Islam. The second factor is that the solution must be organic, which means that it has to be initiated by a Jew or a Muslim Arab citizen of that region who is versed in both, the Holy Qur'an and the Jewish Tanakh. Why? Arabs respect the Holy Qur'an and pious Jews respect the Tanakh. The conflict, at its core, is a quarrel between the followers of the same religion but two different Shari'a (covenants), the Islamic Shari'a (covenant) of the Prophet Muhammad and the Jewish Shari'a (covenant) of the Prophet Moses. The Holy Qur'an says[1] this and the Hadith tradition also say this.

---

1 - In this paper the Middle East is defined to consist of the following countries (Egypt, Israel, Iran, Iraq, Jordan, Lebanon, Palestine, KSA, Syria, Turkey) The Future of the Global Muslim Population. Pew Research Center Retrieved 22 December 2011.
2 - Tawfik Hamid, "Why George Mitchell Failed", Jerusalem Post, May 15, 2011.
3 - Daniel Levy, "Mideast Envoy George Mitchell Resigns, 'Hit A Brick Wall' On Israeli-Palestinian Peace Talks", Huff Post World, May 13, 2011.

Commonalities
AND DIFFERENCES

Both Muslims and Jews worship and revere the same God, the God of Abraham and Moses. Both Muslims and Jews affirm the absolute unity of God. Because the followers of the Prophet Muhammad are the majority in that area, in order to find a lasting peaceful solution to the conflict, one has to respond and alleviate the concerns of the Muslims and render them benign. There is no better way to do that than to exegete the Holy Qur'an in a way that allows for such peace to take place and support such exegesis with historical precedent. In this paper I would like to share with the reader six points supported by Qur'anic verses and Hadith tradition that address the concerns of Muslims. It is not difficult to see that peace would benefit all parties, including multinational U.S. corporations seeking business infrastructure contracts in the global market. With peace at hand, Arab and Jewish human capital, raw material and ingenuity along with American creativity and know-how, can combine to benefit all peoples in the Middle East and beyond. A Middle East with free borders where people can work and live freely along the model of the European Union should contribute positively to world peace and prosperity. A true Biblical jubilee would reign. People would enjoy long-awaited temporal as well as spiritual prosperity. The Holy Qur'an says that the best policy is honesty.[1]

President Obama echoed this Qur'anic sentiment when he

outlined a plan to move forward:

> "In order to move forward, we must say openly to each other the things we hold in our hearts and that too often are said only behind closed doors. There must be a sustained effort to listen to each other; to learn from each other; to respect one another; and to seek common ground . . . It's easier to blame others than to look inward. It's easier to see what is different about someone than to find the things we share. But we should choose the right path, not just the easy path. There's one rule that lies at the heart of every religion -- do unto others as you would have them do unto you." [2]

President Obama is inviting all sides to what scholars term "eminent criticism"[3]. Band-aid solutions no longer work. More attentions must be focused on the causes rather than the symptoms of the conflict. Right diagnosis often leads to right treatments while wrong diagnosis often leads to wrong treatment. This conflict is akin to a patient with abdominal pain whose symptom appears from time to time in the form of skin pimples and pus. The treating physician is busy prescribing medication for the pimples and the pus, which, disappear temporarily to reappear elsewhere on the body. The proper treatment is to focus on medication for the hidden cause of the disease—which may not be seen on the surface—and not to focus on the symptoms, which are all over the news media. To start outlining a possible religious solution to the conflict, one has to look at the plight of the Arab Palestinians and the plight of the Arab Jews[4], then, answer questions like: what is the purpose of the Holy Qur'an? What does the Qur'an say about the plight of both people? What is the concept of Holy Land in the Holy Qur'an? What is dignity and dignitism? This paper will attempt to answer those questions. First, Let us look at the plight of the Palestinian people or Holy Land Arabs on the hands of both the Zionist settlers and the Arab governments.

1 - يَا أَيُّهَا الَّذِينَ آمَنُوا اتَّقُوا اللَّهَ وَكُونُوا مَعَ الصَّادِقِينَ O ye who believe! Fear Allah and be with those who are honest and fruitful. Q9:119
2 - Barak Obama, *"Remarks by the President on a New Beginning"*, Cairo University, Cairo, Egypt, June 4, 2009, On Line.
3 - Longe O, Maratos FA, Gilbert P, Evans G, Volker F, Rockliff H, Rippon G. (2010). Having a word with yourself: Neural correlates of self-criticism and self-reassurance. Neuroimage. 49: 1849–1856.
4 - Arab Jews is a term that refers to Sephardic and Mizrahi Jews who use to live in Arab countries and were uprooted and forced to immigrate to

THE FIRST POINT
THE OPPRESSED OF THE LAND

The first question to be addressed is: what could happen if Arab governments set aside oppression of their own brethren? For example, what could happen if Arab Leaders were to issue a formal apology to their Arab brothers and sisters who were forced to leave the Holy Land "Palestine" in 1948 and 1967 after the creation of the state of Israel? What could happen if Arab governments grant those displaced Holy Land Arabs ("the Oppressed") unconditional full citizenship in all the Arab countries where they reside after having been displaced from their homes and their communities?

According to 1999 survey of the Palestinian refugees, only about 10% of those Holy Land Arabs do not want any other country citizenship;[1] they would like to go back to historical Palestine. However, until they are able to do so they should be offered citizenship in the country of their birth or their current residence. What could happen if Arab governments told the Oppressed, "Sorry, we were wrong in excluding you, your children, and your grandchildren from employment in government, the military, civil service and seventy other professions,"[2] as is the case in at least a dozen Arab countries? What could happen if Arab governments felt guilty of the orchestrated oppression they have been inflicting on those Holy Land Arabs? Why should Arab governments continue to keep those Oppressed Arabs living in deplorable conditions in camps inside the Holy Land such as: Askar,

Balata, Jenin, and Tulkarm, just to name a few?[3] And in twenty-eight camps outside the Holy Land such as Baqa'a, Marka, Shatila and Yarmuk?[4] Arab governments control almost a third of the world's wealth in the form of oil and gas production and reserves, why can't Arab governments make life easier for the Holy Land Arabs?

On the other hand, what could happen if Zionist settlers set aside oppression of their own neighbors? For example, what could happen if Jewish Zionist settlers were to issue a formal apology to their Arab neighbors who lived in the Holy Land for generations before the settlers arrived? What could happen if Zionist settlers grant those displaced Holy Land Arabs ("the Oppressed") unconditional equal treatment where they reside after having been displaced from their homes and their communities? What could happen if the Zionist settlers told the Oppressed, "Sorry, we were wrong in mistreating you, your children, and your grandchildren as is the case in and around all 120 illegal settlements in the West Bank?[5] What could happen if Zionist settlers felt guilty and ashamed of the orchestrated oppression they have been inflicting on those Holy Land Arabs?[6] What could happen if those Zionist settlers uphold the verses in the Tanakh that prohibit mistreating one's neighbor?[7] Why should Zionist settlers continue to keep those Oppressed Arabs living in deplorable conditions in camps inside the Holy Land? Zionist settlers control almost a third of the Israeli Knesset seats, why can't Zionist settlers make life easier for the Holy Land Arabs?

It is rather pathetic that both the Arab and Jewish traditions call for treating the weak and the destitute with magnanimity, love and care;[8] yet Arab governments on one hand and Zionist settlers on the other hand are doing exactly the opposite with the Holy Land Arabs. The number of those oppressed and displaced Holy Land Arabs has grown from 915,000 people in 1950 to more than five million people in 2010.[9]

There are two reasons why the Israeli government will not allow those refugees to return en-mass to the homes for which many of them still have keys. The first reason is that many of those homes are now occupied by Arab Jews who were made to leave—voluntarily or involuntarily—out of the MENA region in the 40's, 50's and 60's. The second reason is that there is general fear among Zionists in Israel that returning refugees may form a fifth column and sow the seed for the destruction of the Jewish state.

In another mockery of justice: the Palestinian Authority—which is funded mainly by US and EU[10]—consider a Palestinian who sells his land to a Jew as having committed treason and therefore is guilty of a capital offense and must face the death penalty.[11] Despite such laws,[12] when some Holy Land Arabs complain about social injustice in the Arab countries, then Arabs add insult to injury.[13] Arabs do that by accusing the Holy Land Arabs of deserving their unbearable conditions in the refugee camps, because they allegedly sold their land to the Jews in Palestine.

Leaving those Holy Land Arabs in refugee camps inside and outside the Holy Land is not without its costs. The physical, emotional and mental suffering sustained by those Holy Land Arabs is exerting psychological pressure on other Arabs from Rabat to Riyadh.[14] Because of the strong tie between Arabs and Muslims—92% of Arabs are Muslims—the pressure on the Arabs is organically influencing one billion Muslims worldwide, from Tangier to Timor. Many of those Muslims started to hate Zionism, Jews and Israel; even though the overwhelming majority of those hating Israel don't even know where Israel exists on a map. I was a witnessed to such hatred among Indian Muslims in as faraway places as Kayalpatnam Mosque, in the State of Tamil Nadu region of India.[15]

Such pressure on Muslims is reflected in the near silence and possible tolerance among Arabs and Muslims of

"Suicide Martyrs" or what is commonly known in the west as "Suicide Bombers" or "Muslim Terrorists". This may be an over simplification, but it appeared to me that while, one group attempts to teach intolerance towards Jews, Zionists and Israel, the other group retaliate by teaching intolerance towards Palestinians, Arabs and Muslims.

---

1 - Khalil Shikaki, RESULTS OF Palestinian Survey Research (PSR) *Refugees' polls in the West Bank / Gaza Strip, Jordan and Lebanon on refugeees' preferences and behavior in a Palstianian-Israelis Permanent Refugee Agreement,* Survey Research

2 - Unit: PSR Polls among Palestinian Refugees, 18 July 2003.

3 - Franklin Lamb, "The Case for Palestinian Right in Lebanon," Counterpunch website, April 20, 2011. 3 - UNRWA: Relief & Social Services Program, Amman Jordan and By William Wheeler, "Palestinians' bittersweet homecoming in Lebanon, *Christian Science Monitor*, 3/5/08. http://www.csmonitor.com/World/Middle-East/2008/0305/p04s01-wome.html

4 - William Wheeler and Don Duncan, *World Politics Review,* March 11, 2008.

5 - Ori Nir, Bankrolling Colonialism, (Jerusalem, Jordan Valley Press, 2010)

6 - Donald Macintyre, "No Changes on Racist Torah's King's Text", The Independent, Jerusalem, May 5, 2012 וַיֹּאמֶר מֹשֶׁה אֶל־הָעָם אַל־תִּירָאוּ

7 - Exodus 20:17 ""You shall not covet your neighbor's Land."

8 - "And they feed, for the love of Allah, the indigent, the orphan, and the captive" Q76:8

9 - UNRWA: Relief & Social Services Program, Amman Jordan.

10 - US and EU fund about half of the PA budget. Fact Sheet: The Palestinian National Authority's Sources of Funding By MIFTAH, February 2006.

11 - Weiner, Justus Reid (2005). Human Rights of Christians in Palestinian Society. Jerusalem Center for Public Affairs. p. 22 and "PA court: Sale of Palestinian land to Israelis is punishable by death", Haarez, Sepember 12, 2010.

12 - Richard S. Levy, (2005). *Anti-Semitism: A historical encyclopedia of prejudice and persecution.* 2. ABC-CLIO. p. 31.

13 - Khaled Abu Toamah, "Contentions, the Palestinians Alone", Commentary, July 12, 2007

14 - Umm Kalthoum Abdu, "Nakba 2011: A Possible Trend-setter for the Upcoming Nakba

15 - In a small mosque called Zawya Shazlia in Kayalpatnam, the name of the 17th chapter of the Holy Qur'an was crossed with a pen and changed from B'nai Israel to Isra. When I asked Abdullah Qasemi the Imam of the Masjid, why the name B'nai Israel was crossed, his answer was "Israel is a bad name".

Radical Islam
AND THE CONFLICT

Solving this problem would eliminate a major grievance that feeds radical extremism throughout the Arab and Islamic worlds.[1] In the West radical Islam is synonymous with terrorism. The dictionary definition of terrorism is: *the use of violence and intimidation in the pursuit of political aims*. When some Arabs—such as the Palestinians—use violence to pursue their political aim of social justice and self determination, Israel calls that terrorism. For which a Zionist Jew may say, no, Palestinians do not want social justice, they want the destruction of the State of Israel. If Palestinians wanted self-determination, they could have had it 31 times since 1937.[2] Their leaders are clear; they want the destruction of Israel.

When some Zionists—such as the Settlers—use violence and intimidation to pursue their political aim of security for Israel through the building of illegal settlements in the West Bank, Arab media call that State Sponsored Terrorism.[3] Incidentally, Arab and Muslim media call the USA drone attacks on Pakistani and Afghani targets as "state sponsored terrorism."[4] Both sides—the Palestinians and the Settlers—are calling each other terrorists. Terrorism is costing the USA dearly. The cost of terrorism (or fear of terrorism) includes long security lines at Airports, metal detectors in all government buildings and general feeling of being unsafe to travel to many parts of the globe. Even USA embassies overseas are looking more and more like castles and garrisons with plenty of security details, guards and even Marines on board. This general feeling of misery on the part of the Holy Land Arabs and the feeling of fear in the West could all become part of history as Ahlul Kitab (Muslims) and Ahlul Kitab religious and political leaders collaborate to resolve this nagging conflict. But we have to start with religious leaders first, once we have an agreement among religious leaders, then we can take it to the political leaders.

It is disheartening to realize that while Arabs claim to be followers of the Prophet Muhammad and his superb Islamic tradition, some Arabs tend to mistreat the weak among them, and use the feeblest of excuses to do so. The Holy Qur'an advise against such practice.[5] What is not an acceptable practice to do with one's own sisters and brothers should also be an unacceptable practice to do with the Holy Land Arabs.[6] Someone may say, but if Arab governments treat the Holy Land Arabs as equal citizens in the land of their host country, Arab governments would dilute the Israeli-Palestinian conflict, and the Holy Land Arabs would forget about going back to their homes in Palestine. Arab governments do not wish to dilute the conflict—they view the State of Israel as an existential threat.[7] So, just like Israel views a Palestinian State next door as an existential threat , Arab governments view a border less Israel as an existential threat.[8] To the Arab governments, if they gave Palestinians their citizenship, Israel will expand and occupy the area between the Nile and the Euphrates (which includes parts of Egypt, parts of KSA, Jordan, Syria, Lebanon and Iraq) as allegedly displayed on the shekel coin, Israeli Knesset, Book of Genesis (15:18) and the Israeli flag.[9] According to a Zionist commentator, there is not a Zionist anywhere in the world who has ever published any claim to any Arab land. Zionists only claim is to the holy land.[10] All or part of it may be under discussion, but nothing more than the Holy Land. The idea of Arab government's who fear that Israel will expand

and conquer more and more until all Arabs of the Middle East are under the control of Israel is beyond absurd. It is a ploy to sow fear in the hearts of their own people.[11] On the other hand it is Israel and Zionism that is being constantly attacked by Arab and Muslim political leaders. For example, Zionists view that Ahmadinejad wants the destruction of Israel—not peace. Hamas wants "resistance till victory or martyrdom"—not peace. Hezbollah's Musawi wants "fighting [the Jews] not because we want something from you (Israel). We are fighting you because we want to destroy you" and Hassan Nasr 'Allah said to the Beirut Star: "we want all the Jews to come to Israel so that we don't need to go after them world-wide".[12] These political leaders do not want peace. They only want Israel's destruction and the annihilation of the Zionist project. To those antagonists, no price is too high, their people's lives, their own countries' economies, nothing too high to pay for the end goal of Israel's destruction.

However, any discussion on the conflict is not complete until one considers the plight of the indigenous people of historical Palestine. Therefore, before one considers the plight of the Arab Jews, it is important to ask the question: who are the Palestinian people and who is the legitimate representative of the Palestinian people?

1 - Alan Berger, Harvey Cox, Herbert C. Kelman, Lenore G. Martin, Everett Mendelsohn, Augustus Richard Norton, Henry Steiner, Stephen M. Walt Israel and Palestine: Two States for Two people, if not now when? Boston Study Group on Middle East Peace.
2 - David Meir Levi, "31 Opportunities for Statehood Squandered in Favor of Genocide", Front Page Magazine, July 15, 2011
3 - Erdoğan accuses Israel of state terrorism, Today's Zaman, June 1, 2010
4 - Craig Mackenzie, U.S. drone strike kills 10 suspected militants in Pakistan as they 'console' family of commander killed in attack the day before, Prison Planet, June 3, 2012
5 - إِنَّمَا الْمُؤْمِنُونَ إِخْوَةٌ فَأَصْلِحُوا بَيْنَ أَخَوَيْكُمْ "The Believers are but a single Brotherhood:" Q49:10 All Qur'anic verses in this paper are done using Abdullah Yûsuf Ali, *The Meaning of the Holy Qur'an* (Maryland: Amana Publications, 2009)
6 - The Prophet of Islam said: مثل المؤمنين في توادهم وتعاطفهم وتراحمهم مثل الجسد إذا اشتكى منه شيء تداعى له سائر الجسد بالسهر والحمى "the likening of the believers in their mutual love, sympathy and mercy is like the body, if a small part is hurting, the whole body reels in fever until that part is healed." Imam Nawawi, Ryadul Saleheen (Cairo: Al Darul Hadith 2010) 65.
7 - Deuteronomy 11:24" "Every place where you set your foot will be yours: Your territory will extend from the desert to Lebanon, and from the Euphrates River to the Mediterranean Sea."
כָּל־הַמָּקוֹם אֲשֶׁר תִּדְרֹךְ כַּף־רַגְלְכֶם בּוֹ לָכֶם יִהְיֶה מִן־הַמִּדְבָּר וְהַלְּבָנוֹן מִן־הַנָּהָר נְהַר־פְּרָת וְעַד הַיָּם הָאַחֲרוֹן יִהְיֶה גְּבֻלְכֶם John Tirman, The "Existential Threat" to Israel Is Israel", Huff Post World, March 3, 2012.
8 - Michael B. Oren, Seven Existential Threats, Commentary, May 2009.
9 - Daniel Pipes, Imperial Israel: The Nile-to-Euphrates Calumny, Middle East Quarterly, March 1994
10 - David Meir-Levi, Zionist Lecturer at San Jose University, via e-mail dated June 13, 2012.
11 - Ibid.
12 - "The Enemy Within", *New York Times*, May 23, 2004.

REPLACE PLO
WITH HLCO

The Palestinian people are the people who inhabited the area between the Mediterranean coast and the Jordan River, commonly known as Palestine. Palestinians are represented in the international community by the Palestine Liberation Organization (PLO), founded in 1964 by the Arab League—the regional organization which now includes 22 Arab states and the PLO.[1] The PLO has a name, a mission and a purpose. From a religious point of view, all three aspects about the PLO are harmful. The name is harmful, the mission is harmful and the purpose is harmful—this is harmful to the PLO far more than it is harmful to the State of Israel. That is why the PLO has not been successful in winning equality and social justice for the Palestinian people inside or outside the Holy Land. Someone might argue that the PLO's goal for social justice or equality was secondary to a more pressing priority: the struggle until victory (destruction of Israel) or martyrdom.[2]

Here is why one may say that: the stated mission of the PLO is to establish a nation state for the people it represents—and control the flow of Jews running away from persecution and prevent them from reaching the Holy Land. The PLO name is harmful because the land on which the PLO aspire to form a State is named in both the Holy Torah and the Holy Qur'an as the Holy Land—not Palestine. The purpose is harmful because the PLO seeks to liberate the Holy Land from the very people who should be in the Holy Land when they have nowhere else to go. If all three aspects about the PLO are harmful, what three aspects may the PLO consider to become benign? The Palestinian Liberation Organization (PLO) may consider to change its name to Holy Land Custodians Organization (HLCO). HLCO is much more beneficial than PLO. Why? The name Holy Land is more consistent with the Holy Scriptures than Palestine. The concept of "Custodian" denotes watching over and keeping and it can also imply serving and protecting the weak. Contrast that with the concept of "Liberating" which may imply war, incarceration and bondage. If Holy Land Arabs focus on guarding, helping and serving others, especially those running away from persecution, we all win. The compelling reason to affect the name change for the PLO would be to stay true to the teachings of the Prophet Muhammad and the Holy Qur'an. God will be pleased that the PLO chose a name, a mission and a purpose that brings it closer to the word of Allah as delineated in the Holy Qur'an. To convince the PLO leadership of the name change one would ask: Do you love Allah? Do you love the Prophet Muhammad? Do you want to draw yourself closer to Allah and His prophet? Yes. Change your name from PLO to HLCO and you will be drawing yourself closer to Allah and His prophet.

Therefore, going back to the Holy Land the Arabs "right of return" must be balanced with the Arab governments' willingness to allow, the scattered Arabs or Sephardic and Mizrahi Jews, who left—voluntarily or involuntarily—to return to their communities. That is, the Holy Land Arabs' right of return has to be balanced against the Arab Jews right of return, which leads us to consider the plight of the Arab Jews, who came to the Holy Land after being kicked out of their countries.

---

1 - Who represents the Palestinians officially before the world community? Institute for Middle East Understanding (IMEU).
2 - Meir-Levi, Zionist Lecturer at San Jose University, via email dated June 13, 2012.

THE SECOND POINT
THE SCATTERED IN THE LAND

"A million Jews live in Egypt [and other Arab countries] and enjoy all the rights of citizenship, they have no desire to emigrate to Palestine. However, if a Jewish State were established no body could prevent disorder. Riots would breakout in Palestine and spread through all the Arab States and may lead to a war between two races." [1]

These were the prophetic comments by Heykal Pasha, member of the Egyptian Delegate to the United Nations in April, 1947. As he predicted a war broke out the following year where it is reported by all possible records that close to half a million Holy Land Arabs were forced to leave, were evacuated or ran away (for safety). As usual, there are two sides to this story. On the Arab side it is reported that the newly established Zionist State in Palestine, caused the persecution and evacuations of those Holy Land Arabs. On the Israeli side, it is reported that those Holy Land Arabs picked up what they could carry with them and left their homes voluntarily to make room for Jews to come and live in Palestine! In Arab circles this event is commemorated annually, on May 15th, as the Palestinian Nakba Day. As a result of the Nakba Jews in Arab Land were affected in a negative way. A retaliatory policy was put in place in the Arab League to drive Arab Jews out of the Arab Land.[2] Following orders issued by the Arab League, outrageous acts were committed against Arab Jews from North Africa, Egypt, Levant, Mesopotamia, and Yemen.[3] For example, the specific discrimination of which the Jews of Yemen complained, which contributed to the exodus from Yemen was the forced Islamization of Jewish Orphans.[4] This is akin to the Christianization of Jewish Orphans that took place in Spain in 1492.[5] In KSA, the Jews of Najran were offered (or forced) to leave the Kingdom on a specific day. On that specific day, KSA soldiers asked the Jews to hand their money over in order to protect it during the journey over land to the border. When the Jews arrived at the border, they asked for their money back. At that point they were told "the money had been confiscated by the Kingdom of Saudi Arabia" for under the Saudi Law it was forbidden to strengthen the State of Israel by money from KSA.[6] In Iraq, Law No. 1 of 1950 deprived Jews of their Iraqi nationality, and law No. 5 of 1951 deprived Iraqi Jews of their property.[7] In Libya, by the time colonel Gaddafi came to power most Libyan Jews had fled the country. However, Gaddafi's immediate mission was to cleanse the nation of the few remaining Jews.[8] In Syria, Jewish property was taken and appropriated and given to Arab refugees from the Holy Land. Holy Land Arabs were placed in houses in the Jewish ghetto in Damascus.[9] In Egypt, Jews, including highly respected members of the community were incarcerated and later were expelled from Egypt by sea and air.[10] In Algeria, a mother of two Jewish boys came back home from shopping to find her two young boys in a pool of blood, their throats cut. This was the final provocation that made the Jews leave Algeria.[11] Mr. Sabri Jiryis, director of the Institute of Palestine Studies in Beirut, summarized the condition of Arab Jews in an article published in the Beirut Daily AL-Nahar on May 15, 1975:

> *"The State of Israel will raise the question in all serious negotiations that may in time be conducted over the rights of the Palestinians . . . Israel argument will take approximately the following form: it is true that we Israeli's brought about the exodus of the Arabs from their land in Palestine in the war of 1948 . . . and that we took control of their property [and appropriated it to the Jews]. In return, however, you Arabs caused the expulsion of a like number of Jews from Arab countries since 1948. Most of them went to Israel after you seized control of their property one way or another. What happened is merely a kind of 'population and property transfer', the consequence of which both sides have to bear."*

Given the above unpleasant history of Arab governments treatment of their own citizens, the Arab Jews, What could happen if Arab governments consider the waves of Jewish people who came to the Holy Land in the 1940s and 1950s as people running away from danger, as people tired of oppression and subjugation, as people looking for self-determination—a place in the sun? What could happen if Arab governments thought that the Jews were persecuted in Europe with nowhere else to go? What would happen if Arab governments finally acknowledge and believe that the Holocaust actually happened—and that in it one-third of all Jews vanished?[12] What could happen if Arabs and Jews put into practice the ethical and moral values contained in their respective sacred text and forgave each other?[13]

While the Sephardic Jews came to the Holy Land because they were forced out—voluntarily or involuntarily—by Arab government in retaliation for the exodus of the Holy Land Arabs, the Ashkenazi Jews came to the Holy Land because they were persecuted and killed by the Nazi war machine in Europe in a horrific process called the Holocaust. Entire Jewish communities were annihilated in Germany, Poland, Russia, and other European countries. Now, the Jews are not unified as to how to explain the Holocaust. To the Orthodox Jews the Holocaust is a message from God to shun secular life. To the Zionist Jews the Holocaust is a message from God that Palestine must be made a Jewish home land—by force if necessary. To the secular Jews the Holocaust is a message that God is not in control or God does not exist.[14] Last summer, on a trip to Kiev, Ukraine, I was a witness to one of those WW2 horror stories; on a visit to Babi Yar, where on Yom Kippur in 1941 the Nazis, methodically murdered more than 33,000 Jewish men, women, and children.[15] The Jews came to the Holy Land running away from danger. They came to take shelter among their cousins the Arab descendents of Ismail. Allah put in the heart of the Jews that there was no safer place for the Jews to go except the Holy Land. Furthermore, Allah put in the hearts of some Christians (once the arch enemies of the Jews) the desire—out of guilt and remorse—for what happened at the Holocaust, to support the Jewish people in their endeavor for safety and security.

1 - Heykal Pasha, *Official Records of The Second Session of The General Assembly, Ad Hoc Committee on the Palestinian Question, Summary Record of Meetings,* United Nations, 25 September to 25 November 1947, Lake Success, New York, Page 185. As quoted by, Ya'Akov Meron, *The Forgotten Millions: The Modern Jewish Exodus from Arab Lands,* (New York: Continuum, 1999) Page 84.
2 - Ibid page 83.
3 - H. J. Cohn, the Jews of The Middle east, 1860-1972, (Jerusalem: Israel University Press, 1973) page 67
4 - Ibid page 64.
5 - Arthur Benveniste , "500th Anniversary of the Forced Conversion of the Jews of Portugal", From an address at Sephardic Temple Tifereth Israel, Los Angeles, October 1997
6 - Ibid page 86.
7 - Ibid page 87.
8 - Ibid page 91.
9 - Ibid page 92.
10 - Ibid page 93
11 - Ibid page 93
12 - "In 1939, there were 17 million Jews in the world, and by 1945 only 11 million. "Ner Le Elef, World Jewish Population. http://www.simpletoremember.com/vitals/world-jewish-population.htm#_ftn1
13 - Allah said:

وَلَقَدْ أَخَذَ اللَّهُ مِيثَاقَ بَنِي إِسْرَائِيلَ وَبَعَثْنَا مِنْهُمُ اثْنَيْ عَشَرَ نَقِيبًا وَقَالَ اللَّهُ إِنِّي مَعَكُمْ لَئِنْ أَقَمْتُمُ الصَّلَاةَ وَآتَيْتُمُ الزَّكَاةَ وَآمَنْتُم بِرُسُلِي وَعَزَّرْتُمُوهُمْ وَأَقْرَضْتُمُ اللَّهَ قَرْضًا حَسَنًا لَأُكَفِّرَنَّ عَنكُمْ سَيِّئَاتِكُمْ وَلَأُدْخِلَنَّكُمْ جَنَّاتٍ تَجْرِي مِن تَحْتِهَا الْأَنْهَارُ فَمَن كَفَرَ بَعْدَ ذَٰلِكَ مِنكُمْ فَقَدْ ضَلَّ سَوَاءَ السَّبِيلِ فَبِمَا نَقْضِهِم مِّيثَاقَهُمْ لَعَنَّاهُمْ وَجَعَلْنَا قُلُوبَهُمْ قَاسِيَةً يُحَرِّفُونَ الْكَلِمَ عَن مَّوَاضِعِهِ وَنَسُوا حَظًّا مِّمَّا ذُكِّرُوا بِهِ وَلَا تَزَالُ تَطَّلِعُ عَلَىٰ خَائِنَةٍ مِّنْهُمْ إِلَّا قَلِيلًا مِّنْهُمْ ۖ فَاعْفُ عَنْهُمْ وَاصْفَحْ ۚ إِنَّ اللَّهَ يُحِبُّ الْمُحْسِنِينَ

Allah (swt) did aforetime take a covenant with the Children of Israel; and We raised up from among them twelve chieftains. And Allah (swt) said, 'I am with you. Surely, if you perform the prayer, and = pay the alms, and believe in My Messengers, honour and assist them, and loan to Allah a beautiful loan, verily I will wipe out from you your evils, and admit you to gardens with rivers flowing beneath; but if any of you, after this, resisteth faith, he hath truly wandered from the path or rectitude. But because of their breach of their covenant, We cursed them, and made their hearts grow hard; they change the words from their (right) places and forget a good part of the message that was sent them, nor wilt thou cease to find them ever bent on (new) deceits, except a few of them. Yet pardon them, and forgive; surely Allah (swt) loves the good-doers". (al-Maeda 5,12-16)
14 - James Carroll, Constantine's Sword: The Church and the Jews (New York, Houghton Mifflin Company, 2001) p 6.
15 - Omer Salem, Notes From the Quad, an alumni e-Magazine Yale Divinity School, in the summer of 2011.

Brief History
OF THE JEWS

The story of the Jews being outnumbered by their antagonists and running away from persecution has many precedents in history. The Jewish Exodus story started in Egypt, followed with the Assyrian Enslavement, the Babylonian Exile, the Greek Occupation, the Roman destruction, the French Crusades, the English Expulsion, the Spanish Inquisition, the Russian Pogroms and culminating with the German Holocaust. So let us look at the last time the Jews were expelled from a European country—the Spanish Inquisition. Where did the Jews go? Where did the Jews run for cover? Where did they hide from danger? In Arab and Muslim lands. In 1492, when the Jews were persecuted and faced annihilation, at the hand of Ferdinand and Isabella, on the Iberian Peninsula during the Spanish Inquisition, they fled to North Africa, Egypt, the Levant, Mesopotamia, and Anatolia. In 1492, Arabs and Muslims faced the same dilemma they are facing today. Namely, what to do with the Jews?[1] But did the Arabs oppose the Jews back then? Did they incite hatred against the Jews? Did they slaughter the Jews or pledge to feed the Jews to the fish in the sea? No! Arabs and Muslims back then, sheltered the Jews, comforted the Jews, and made the Jews members of their society. Arabs and Muslims healed the wounds suffered by the Jews at the hands of the Spaniards.

One might ask, if that is true about the Muslims of the Ottoman Empire, how come many of the Contemporary Muslims hate Israel? Contemporary Muslims hate Israel, not because it offers a shelter for Jews running away from danger and not because it is a socialist and democratic nation. Contemporary Muslims hate Israel, because they view Israel as a colonial powerhouse that descended on the Palestinian people, not to share the Holy Land, but to cleanse the Holy Land from all non-Jews—by force if necessary. According to Benjamin Abrahamson, a religious judge and scholar in Israel "the fundamental difference between the Ottoman acceptance of Jewish refugees and the Zionist attempt to found a state was that under the Ottoman's the Jews were viewed as co-religionists not as foreigners."[2]

Now let's think about this: Were those Arabs and Muslims—who helped the Jews in 1492— mentally sluggish? Did they lack intelligence or good judgment when they provided shelter for the fleeing Jews? Were they not aware of the Holy Qur'an and Hadith traditions of the Prophet Muhammad? In fact, those Arabs were quite aware of the Qur'an and Hadith. They were actually wiser than the Arabs of the 1940s and 1950s, and they exercised good judgment. In fact, they used the Qur'an and Hadith as a basis to host and show integrity, kindness, and magnanimity to the Jews who were running away from danger on the Iberian Peninsula. The Arabs were relying on Allah's commandments in the Holy Qur'an to provide the most precious commodity for those running away from persecution and danger—security.[3] "Security" is what the Spanish Jews were looking for five centuries ago when they fled to Arab land, and security is what the Jews are looking for today when they flee to Arab land. With the Jews, history seems to repeats itself. This time the Jews are seeking security in our shared Holy Land. The majority of the Jews who came to the Holy Land are willing to share it with the Holy Land Arabs—only a small minority wants the whole land for only the Jews. On the other hand, the majority of the Holy Land Arabs are willing to share the Holy Land with the Jews—only a small minority wants the whole land for only the Arabs.

---

1 - David D. Freedman, "Legal Systems Very Different From Our Own", May 18, 2006
2 - Benjamin Abrahamson, Religious Court Judge in Jerusalem, Israel, via email dated May 15, 2012.
3 - "If a non-Muslim asks you for asylum, grant it to him, so that he may hear the word of Allah. Then escort him to where he will be secure." Q9:6..

The Nature
OF THE CONFLICT

This is why in contemporary Western mainstream media, the adjective most associated with the Jews is "security," as in "the security of Jews" or "the security of Israel." Even when the fourth largest army in the world (Israel) was bombarding Gaza in 2009, it was under the pre-text of "the security of Israel". The security of Israel has been used as a pre-text to commit a mascara in Gaza where twelve-hundreds Arabs, mostly women and children were killed. Who to blame for that? The State of Israel and its desire for security or the Arab governments and their desire for dominance? What is amazing about this sixty seven-year-old conflict between Arabs and Jews is that both sides of the conflict are talking about a different cause. The Palestinians who live in the Holy Land are struggling for dignity and social justice, and the Jews who came to the Holy Land are struggling for safety and security. Arabs and Jews have two entirely different objectives. The Arabs are suing for dignity whereas the Jews are suing for security. Is that dichotomy clear? The conflict is not entirely about the control of land. The conflict may include land, but the conflict is not entirely about land. The conflict can thus be summarized as **Jewish security vs. Arab dignity.** Some would say, the conflict is also about geopolitical interest for the USA and EU members; however, such interest can be attained away from the conflict. This really means that if Arab governments truly want dignity for the Holy Land Arabs, then

Arab governments should find a way to restore the security for the Jews. If one understands that, one could find a way to afford the Holy Land Jews their security while affording the Holy Land Arabs their dignity. Moreover, despite the fact that some Arab Palestinians like Hamas leaders make fiery speeches[1] about their desire to destroy the Zionist state, they are really fighting to live in dignity next to the Zionist State.[2] This leads to a very important point to make about the Jews in Arab lands.

---

1 - The armed resistance and the armed struggle are the path and the strategic choice for liberating the Palestinian land, from the [Mediterranean] sea to the [Jordan] river, and for the expulsion of the invaders and usurpers [Israel] . . . We won't relinquish one inch of the land of Palestine." Hamas leader in the Gaza Strip Ismail Haniyeh, The Western Center for Journalism, December 28, 2011

2 - Jimmy Carter, "Don't Give Up on Mideast Peace", *New York Times*, April 12,

THE JEWS
IN ARAB LAND

"Arabs didn't call themselves Palestinians until the Zionist movement began and Jews did not call themselves Israelis until the establishment of the state of Israel." [1]

There are many perspectives on how the State of Israel came to existence in Palestine. The State of Israel emerged from interaction with "the reality of war in Europe and Jews collective memory of being scattered people seeking a homeland."[2] While, the Zionists see the Holocaust as an organizing rational for the State of Israel,[3] the international community view the 1947 partition plan as the basis for the creation on the State of Israel. Now, let's think about what the State of Israel has consisted of since its inception in 1948: it consisted of Ashkenazi Jews and Sephardic Jews, about 50/50. Now, where did the Sephardic (or Mizrahi) Jews who reside now in the Holy Land come from? They came from Arab lands. They are Arab Jews who came from North Africa, Egypt, Levant, Mesopotamia, and Yemen. Some Jews left Arab lands voluntarily to go to the Holy Land. However, the overwhelming majority of Jews in Arab lands loved their countries and did not want to leave;[4] they had lived there for many generations (in some cases more than 2500 years), and their parents, grandparents, and great-grand parents are all buried there. The overwhelming majority of Jews in Arab lands were actually driven out against their will! The reasons for the involuntary exit of Jews from Arab land included push factors such as persecution, anti-Semitism and political instability, together with pull factors, such as the desire to fulfill Zionist yearnings or find a better economic and secure home in Europe or the Americas. A significant proportion of Jews left due to political insecurity and the rise of Arab nationalism and later also due to policies of some Arab governments that sought to present the expulsion of Jews as a crowd-driven retaliatory act for the exodus of Arab refugees from Palestine.[12]

Now, let's stop for a moment and see what some Arabs did to their Arab sisters and brothers (some of whom happened to be Jewish), who lived in safety within Arab countries, within Arab communities, and were citizens of Arab countries and neighbors in Arab lands. What did Arab governments do to the Jews? For the most parts, Arab governments uprooted them, and kicked them out. In fact, about one million Jews had to leave Arab lands involuntarily.[6] Arab governments confiscated their places of worship, took away their communities and possessions and threw them out of Arab countries. One must acknowledge that Zionist sympathizes among Arab Jews incited some Jews to leave Arab countries and not all Arabs approved of such treatment of the Jews. However, this action by Arab governments in the 1950s and 1960s is contrary to the commandments of Allah and his messenger in the Holy Qur'an. An excuse one could find for such action is that Arab governments were still affected and influenced by colonial powers and Zionism was on the rise at that time.[7] Now, one is not saying that all the affected Arab Jews were angels and that none of them did anything wrong such as spying for Israel. Rather, one is saying that the wrong-doers could have been dealt with separately. The Prophet Muhammad warned believers against collective punishment for the sins of a few in the Holy Qur'an:[8] And thus the Prophet of Allah warned against the cry of the oppressed.[9] And the renowned Muslim scholar Taqi ad-Din Ahmad ibn Taymiyyah (d. 1328) echoed the same notion when he declared that "The just nation prevails even if ruled by non-Muslim while the oppressor nation vanishes, even if ruled by Muslim."[10] The Hebrew Bible also warns against collective punishment.[11] Therefore, any collective punishment portrayed by the Arab governments against Arab Jews is a transgression against God. And any collective punishment portrayed by the Zionist settlers against Holy Land Arabs is also a transgression against God. Both sides claim that they are the rightful decedents of Abraham. Both sides claim that God gave them the land, yet, both sides are transgressing against the same God—who gave them the land. That is why peace in lost in the Holy Land.

Given the treatment of Arab Jews described above, couldn't one think that an acknowledgment that Arab governments may have unjustly expelled[11] the Jews would soften the hearts of people on both sides of the conflict over the Holy Land? Then, going further, Arab governments could astound everyone by making an unconditional invitation to those Jews who were mistreated and eased out—voluntarily or involuntarily—to return to their communities and synagogues in Arab lands as protected people and not as an oppressed minority, as equal citizens of the land, not as second or third-class citizens. Such move will encourage the government of Israel to reciprocate and treat the Holy Land Arabs who live and work in Israel, not as second class citizens, but as equal citizens of the land. Why? The law of reciprocity is an integral part of the Bible.[12]

The notion of welcoming back Arab Jews into Arab land, while the State of Israel occupies the Holy Land may be viewed by some Arabs as a bad idea. It may be viewed as "having it both ways". It is regarded that way, because, the Shas party (which consists mainly of Arab Jews) is viewed as the main oppressor of the Holy Land Arabs. Therefore, how could one welcome the oppressors of fellow Arabs back into Arab Lands?

One could argue however that it is in the best interest of both Arab governments and the State of Israel to explore such option. On the Jewish side there are three factors, which detract from such options. **Firstly**, the standard of living of the Jews in Israel is higher than it was in their former countries. In fact, it is often said that many Holy Land Arabs would prefer to live in the State of Israel than in a sovereign Palestinian state.[13] While that may be true, some Jews would rather live in the country of their ancestors. Some Jews also have a troubled conscious because of the way Holy Land Arabs are treated in the State of Israel and they would rather go to a country where everyone is treated equally.[14] After all, money is not everything. The Tanakh teaches that better is a little income with righteousness than great income with injustice.[15] Arab Jews may reason that it makes perfect sense to move to say Egypt or Morocco and have trade links between Israel and those states. As Jonathan Sacks, the chief rabbi of the United Hebrew Congregations of the Commonwealth mentions that each one of us has something someone else needs, and each one of us needs something someone else has, we gain by interaction [and we lose by conflict]. Such interaction is what makes trade the most compelling counter force to conflict.[16]

Secondly, one of the fears of the Zionist Jews is assimilation. As to the assimilation of Jews into Arab society, no need to worry about that either. The most famous of the Israelite monarchs, King David, is claimed to be a descendent of Ruth a non-Jew. Also in modern times, the most famous Jew, who died in the Holocaust, making her diary an international best seller, Anne Frank, comes from an assimilated family.[17] While some Jews might see that living in close proximity with each other in the State of Israel gives them hope of a resurrected national identity. It is also important to realize that it is not wise to put all one's eggs in one basket. Having Jews living in their ancestor's communities in those Arab countries will foster mutual trust and build channels of trade between the State of Israel and those Arab regions. The return of Jews to Arab lands would be a trust building step that is consistent with the Holy Qur'an message.[18] There is much precedence in history of building trust between Muslims and non-Muslims by giving equal status to *dhimmi*[19] subjects in Muslim majority states, starting with the Medina Charter[20] of the Prophet Muhammad, the Ott Katti Sharif reform[21] of the Ottoman Empire, and the Montefiore Edict of Toleration in Morocco.[22] Why would this be good for everyone? It would show that Arab governments have the confidence to face the truths of the past without fear. It would give Arab peoples a clear conscience and make them feel good that they stand on high moral ground.

Thirdly, the return of Arab Jews to Arab Lands may be viewed negatively by some Zionists. Why? Some Zionists would like to create a Jewish, ethnically pure, area in Palestine. Zionists are spending considerable resources to attract Jews to come to the Holy Land and live there permanently. Therefore, the main objection to the return of Arab Jews to Arab lands may be, not the Arab governments, but the Zionists.

THE **STRUGGLE** FOR THE HOLY LAND

1 - Bob Anschuetz, "Let's End Our Wars on the "Other": U.S. Interests, Israeli Fears, and the Demonization of Iran", Tikkun Magazine: To heal, repair and transform the world, January 2, 2012.
2 - Ellen Lust, the Middle East (Washington DC: CQ Press, 2011) page 460.
3 - James Carroll, Constantine's Sword: The Church and the Jews (New York, Houghton Mifflin Company, 2001) p 5.
4 - Prof. Ada Aharoni , The Forced Migration of Jews from Arab Countries and Peace, The Ben Gurion University in Beer Shiva, Dept of Education, 7.5.2004
5 - Malka Hillel Shulewitz, The Forgotten Millions: The Modern Jewish Exodus from Arab Lands, (London: Continuum 2001).
6 - "Zionism is a form of nationalism for Jews and Jewish culture . . . [that] support Jews upholding their Jewish identity and opposes the assimilation of Jews into other societies and has advocated the return of Jews to The State of Israel as a means for Jews to be liberated from anti-Semitic discrimination, exclusion, and persecution that has occurred in other societies." Werner Bergmann, Rainer Erb, Belinda Cooper, "Anti-Semitism in Germany", (New Jersey: Transaction Publishers, 1997)
7 - Ibidem Q17:15: وَلَا تَزِرُ وَازِرَةٌ وِزْرَ أُخْرَىٰ وَمَا كُنَّا مُعَذِّبِينَ حَتَّىٰ نَبْعَثَ رَسُولًا nor can the bearer of a burden bear the burden of another, nor do We chastise until We raise a messenger." And Q4:105. الدولة العادلة تسود و ان كانت كافرة والدولة الظالمة تندثر ولو كانت مؤمنة.
8 - Imam Nawawi, Ryadul Saleheen (Cairo: Hadith Publications, 2009) 67. اتق دعوة المظلوم ولو كان كافراتقبل دعوته وعليه كفر Be careful of the prayer of the oppressed. Even if the oppressed is not a Muslim, his prayer will be answered in this life and he will be judged about his faith in the next life."
9 - Ibn Taymihhah, fatawi Ibn Taymyyah, (2001: Cairo Press volume 4, page 26.)
10 - Deuteronomy 24:16 לֹא־יוּמְתוּ אָבוֹת עַל־בָּנִים וּבָנִים לֹא־יוּמְתוּ עַל־אָבוֹת אִישׁ בְּחֶטְאוֹ יוּמָתוּ Parents are not to be put to death for their children, nor children put to death for their parents; each will die for their own sin."
11 - "According to Professor Ya'akov Meron, who ia an Expert in Islamic Law and has a vast knowledge of the Arab world, the [Jews] were expelled" Malka Hillel Shulewitz, "The Forgotten Millions: the Modern Jewish Exodus from Arab Land", (London: Continuum, 2000) page xvi.
12 - Whatever is disagreeable to yourself do not do unto others. (Shayast-na-Shayast 13:29)
13 - Daniel Pipers, "The Hell of Israel is Better then the Paradise of Arafat", Middle East Quarterly, Spring 2005, p 43.
14 - Occupation, Colonialism, Apartheid. "Democracy and Governance Program", Middle East Project May 2009.
15 - Proverb16:8 טוֹב־מְעַט בִּצְדָקָה מֵרֹב תְּבוּאוֹת בְּלֹא מִשְׁפָּט
16 - Jonathan Sacks, *The Dignity of Difference* (London: Continuum Publishing, 2002) p. 15
17 - Joseph Tuelushkin, Jewish Literacy (New York: William Morrow and Company, 1991) p 367.
18 - Allah said: وَإِنْ أَحَدٌ مِنَ الْمُشْرِكِينَ اسْتَجَارَكَ فَأَجِرْهُ حَتَّىٰ يَسْمَعَ كَلَامَ اللَّهِ ثُمَّ أَبْلِغْهُ مَأْمَنَهُ If a non-Muslim asks you for asylum, grant it to him, so that he may hear the word of Allah. Then escort him to where he will be secure." Q9:6.
19 - *Dhimmi* is the Arabic name for non-Muslims living in Muslim-ruled land.

20 - A. Guillaume, *The Life of Muhammad — A Translation of Ishaq's Sirat Rasul Allah*, Oxford University Press, Karachi, 1955; pp. 231–233.
21 - Norman Stillman, The Jews of Arab Land (Philadelphia: The Jewish Publication Society, 1979) p 97. The Katt-i Sharif: enumeration of reforms that affected the individual subjects of the Ottoman Empire. It echoed many of the libertarian ideals that had been voiced in the French Declaration of the Rights of Man.
22 - Norman Stillman, Ibid., p 100. On February 5, 1864, Mawlay Muhammad issued a dahir, or royal decree, declaring his intention to treat his Jews with complete justice as was due any Moroccan subject and to protect them from all oppression.

OBJECTIONS
TO REPATRIATION

Generally speaking, Arab politicians do not have a problem with the repatriation of Arab Jews.[1] It is Arab religious leaders that need to be convinced—using the Holy Qur'an—of the value of such repatriation. The challenges religious leaders may face are with the radical Muslim groups and the way they exegete the Holy Qur'an to say that Jews are infidels[2] and, therefore, prevent the Jews from returning to Arab land. They also disapprove of Jews having a home land in Palestine. The following section delineates the top-ten religious and non-religious objections leveled by powerful Arab clerics[3] to Jews' returning to and reclaiming their communities in Arab countries. Included here as well, Qur'anic answers to those objections, which are often concealed deliberately from the masses or misquoted to keep the conflict alive. The conflict allows Arab regimes to hold on to power and justify anti-Semitism.

---

1 - Joshua Teitelbaum, "The Arab Peace Initiative", (Jerusalem: Jerusalem Center for Public Affairs, 2009)
2 - Yaser Burhami, "Jews and Christens are Infidels", El Masry Elyoum, December 25, 2011, page 3.
3 - Powerful Muslim Arab clerics have a gridlock on the hearts and minds of the majority of the people in the Middle East. This is not a speculative claim. Religious clerics such as Yacoub, Hassan, Burhami or Howaini in Egypt, Hussain of Palestine or Abdul Aziz Al al-Shaikh of KSA who made a recent Fatwa to demolish all non-Muslim places of worship in KSA have tremendous influence on the masses. They can issue assassination fatwas that will be carried out by their adherents as was the case with the late president Sadat.

JEWS & ARAB
ENMITY

First objection: someone might say,[1] but the Qur'an says the Jews are the enemies of the believers; the Jews killed Allah's prophets.[2] How can someone ask us to allow the enemies of Allah[3] to return to the land? Are you out of your mind? There are two points to make here: firstly, if the Jews killed the prophets of Allah, where did those prophets of Allah go after they were killed? If those killed prophets were false prophets, then they were misleading the people and they received their punishment as commanded in the Holy Qur'an[4] and the Torah.[5] However, if those prophets of Allah were true, then according to the Holy Qur'an they went to heaven. In addition, Allah told us in the Holy Qur'an to treat our enemies with *Ihsan*[6], which is to say with kindness, integrity, and respect (dignitism). And Allah said: kindness will be met with kindness, integrity will be met with integrity and respect will be met with respect.[7] And even if Arabs hate the Jews because of some narrative Arabs have heard or read, or because of 60 years of bitter history, Allah warns the believers against failing to treat a person with integrity, even if one hates that person.[8] Actually, according to the Qur'an, the Jews, like any other people, can be the best people who have ever lived[9], or the they can be the worst.[10] Allah said that the Jews will be with us to the end of time. If Muslim or Christian religious leaders think that the Jews will abandon Judaism and convert to Christianity or Islam, they are deluding themselves and they will be disappointed.

In a recent book by, Benzion Netanyahu, the late father of the current Israeli Prime Minster, Netanyahu argues that the *converses*—the Jews who converted to Christianity in Spain—were killed by the thousands for allegedly practicing Judaism in secret. Netanyahu argues that those Jews were actually practicing Christianity. The Spaniards extermination of those Jews came from a deep anti-Semitism not from religious persecution.[11] Netanyahu is clearly advising his fellow Jews that even conversion will not save you from the sword—hence, stand fast as a Jew, do not convert. Therefore, it is good to know how to accept the Jews for what they are, not for what a Muslim or a Christian religious leader wishes they were. It is good to bring out the best in a Jew and avoid the worst.

---

1 - Who is this "someone"? The term "someone" is used to refer to certain Muslim clerics, some of whom are described in the above endnote. They do not use a pen to write or a sword to fight, yet they have a much more lethal and loathed weapon—their tongues.

2 - Q5:82 "Certainly you will find the most violent of people in enmity for those who believe (to be) the Jews and those who are polytheists."

3 - "Here at Yale University common Hall, on November 8, 2012, we had an annual banquet to celebrate the Muslim Festival of Eidul Adha. MSA and the Chaplain's office at Yale chose Provost Salovey to give the key note speech. After the event a Muslim Arab student at Yale came to me in anger: 'MSA made bad choice by having a Jew give the keynote speech' and he invoked Qur'anic text vilifying the Jews; he was then reminded of the Qur'an concept of mercy, he said that mercy only applied to Muslims; and when one attempted to defend MSA for making that choice, one was accused of not being a good Muslim"

4 - Ibid Q5:33 "The punishment of those who wage war against Allah and His Messenger, and strive with might and main for mischief through the land is: execution, or crucifixion"

5 - Deuteronomy 18:20-22: "But a prophet who presumes to speak in my name anything I have not commanded, or a prophet who speaks in the name of other gods, is to be put to death."

6 - Ibid. Q41:34: "Nor can goodness and Evil be equal. Repel (Evil) with what is better: Then the person with whom you have enmity will become your friend and intimate!"

7 - Ibid. Q55:60: "Is the reward of goodness aught but goodness?"

8 - Ibid. Q5:8: "O ye who believe! Stand out firmly for Allah, as witnesses to fair dealing, and let not the hatred of others to you (or your hatred of others) cause you to wrong others and to depart from integrity. Have integrity: that is next to piety: and fear Allah, for Allah is well-acquainted with all that you do."

9 - Ibid. Q45:16: "And certainly We gave the Book and the wisdom and the prophecy to the children of Israel, and We gave them of the goodly things, and We made them excel the nations."
10 - Ibid. Q5:60: "Say: Shall I inform you of (him who is) worse than this in retribution from Allah? (Worse is he) whom Allah has cursed and brought His wrath upon, and of whom He made apes and swine, and he who served the Shaitan; these are worse in place and more erring from the straight path."
11 - Benzion Netanyahu, The Origins of the Inquisition in Fifteenth Century Spain, (New York: The New York Review of Books, 2001) p65

DIGNITISM
AS A PATH TO PEACE

Now, there are ways that encourage the Jews to become good neighbors, and there are ways to ensure that the Jews will become our worst enemies. Arab governments do not lose anything by helping the Jews become the best neighbors to have. One can do that, by treating the Jews with dignitism, which is respect, kindness, and integrity.

If Arabs treat the Jews with dignitism *(Ihsan)*: respect, kindness and integrity, Allah may put in the heart of the Jew to forgive all the wrongs perpetrated on the Jews by others. If the Jews forgive and ask forgiveness, the Jews will be the best human beings that have ever lived. Why? The Jews have a long history of persecution and subjugation to forgive—more than do Christians or Muslims. Moreover, when one hates and treats people with dishonor or disrespect, one inevitably bring out the worst in those people, regardless of their chosen religious tradition. In the Qur'an, Allah said, *"Ihsan* will be met with *Ihsan."* If one says yes, we will do *Ihsan*, but not with the Jews, then one is changing the word of Allah. Allah wants Muslims to practice, perform, and implement *Ihsan* with everyone, Muslim and non-Muslim.[1]

Secondly, we Arabs and Muslims are guilty of the same offence we accuse our Jewish brothers and sisters of doing, namely the killing of prophets. Why? The prophet Muhammad is reported to have said: "the learned ulama (scholars) of my Ummah are akin to the prophets of B'nai Israel".[2] In that

Hadith, the Ulama of the Islamic nation are the equivalent of the prophets of B'nai Israel. That being the case, history tells us that we Muslims have killed many ulama and Khulafa including some of the greatest heirs to the Prophet Muhammad such as Omar Ibnul Khattab, Othman Ibn Affan, Talha, Zubair, Ali Ibn Abi Taleb, Al Hussain Ibn Ali, Al Hassan Ibn Ali and many others.

---

1 - Ibid. Q60:8.
2 - Al Zarkashy, the Pearls of famous Hadith, volume 1, page 167.
 This Hadith is often cited as "Ulama are the inheritors of Anbi'a (prophets)"

JEWS
AS NEIGHBORS

Second objection: someone else might say, "How can we have Jews as our neighbors, in the same town? Did not the Prophet Muhammad drive the Jews out of Medina?" Well, the Prophet Muhammad may have expelled some people who were accused of wrongdoing, irrespective of their faith.[1] However, he accepted Jews as his neighbors in Medina and was married to a Jewish woman, the mother of the believers: *Safiyyah bint Huyayy*,[2] furthermore; a Jew named *Avi Shachm* in Medina kept his shield in trust.[3] According to John Esposito, the Prophet Muhammad himself engaging in dialogue with the Christians of Najran, resulting in a mutually agreeable relationship whereby the Najranis were permitted to pray in the Prophet's Mosque in Medina.[4] In 644, it is narrated that the Muslim Caliphate 'Umar ibn al-Khattab (RA) decided to bring seventy Jewish families back to Jerusalem after all Jews had been expelled from the Holy Land under Byzantine Christian rule.[5] In 1187, when the Muslim sultan and warrior Saladin conquered Jerusalem and retook it from the crusaders, he brought back the Jews who were banned by Christian rulers from living or worshipping in Jerusalem.[6] Also, during the Muslim rule of Spain (750 AD to 1250 AD) interfaith harmony was at exemplary levels. *Convivencia* (living together) in respect and honor prevailed in Spain, not only among Muslims but also among Muslims, Christians and Jews. Such honor and mutual respect reached levels, which appear to be outstanding in today's Middle East. For example: Samuel Ha-Levi (d. 1056), later known as Samuel Ha-Nagid ("the prince"), was the political head of the Jews of Granada in the 11th Century. Ha-Levi quickly rose through the notable ranks to the position of vizier and concilor to the King. When King Habbus died, his son King Muzafar Nasir who also favored Ha-Levi replaced him. In addition to his position as vizier, Ha-Levi was appointed commander of the King's Muslim armies. Samuel and his son, Joseph, were given command over the Muslim army. Ha-Levi led the Muslim army in eighteen years of constant warfare and was killed on the battlefield.[7]

---

1 - W. N Arafat, "New Light on the Story of Banu Qurayza and the Jews of Medina," *Journal of the Royal Asiatic Society of Great Britain and Ireland,* (1976), pp. 100-107.
2 - Sirat Ibn Hisham, (Cairo: Sirah Publications, 2008) volume 5, p. 20.
3 - Ibid., volume 6, p. 26.
4 - John Esposito: what everyone needs to know about Islam (New York: Oxford University Press, 2011) p84.
5 - Norman A. Stillman, The Jews of Arab Land: A History and Source Book (Jewish Publications Society, 1979)
6 - John Esposito: what everyone needs to know about Islam (New York: Oxford University Press, 2011) p88.
7 - Jerusalem Connections Writers Archives, who is who in history of Sephardim.

ONLY
SEEK ALLAH

Third objection: someone else might say, but Allah said that Jews and Christians would never be satisfied with the Prophet Muhammad, no matter what the Prophet Muhammad might do for them, unless he follows their cult.[1] Yes, you are right, Allah said that neither the Jews nor the Christians will be happy with the Prophet Muhammad until he follows their precepts of their culture, therefore, O' Muhammad, do not seek their satisfaction. O' Muhammad, only seek the satisfaction of Allah. Why? If you follow the precepts of the Jews, the Christians will be unhappy with you, and if you follow the precepts of the Christians, the Jews will be unhappy with you. For example, to satisfy the Jews, you have to reject Jesus Christ as God and the Trinity, which are central to Christian belief, and to satisfy Christians, you have to uphold the Trinity and the deity of Jesus Christ, which are unacceptable to Jews. Therefore, O' Muhammad, you can never make both Jews and Christians, simultaneously satisfied with you. Therefore, give up seeking to satisfy the Jews and the Christians, because doing so is impossible. Just be a Muslim the way the Patriarch Abraham taught, and let Jews be Jews and Christians be Christians. Only seek the satisfaction and acceptance of Allah by inviting Jews and Christians to follow the truth that was revealed to you or invite the Jews and Christians to follow the truth that were revealed to them.[2] A key distinction to highlight here is the difference between Deen (basic religion) and Shari'a (covenant). This is taught throughout the Qur'an and Hadith, and it was made into a political reality by the Ottoman Empire. There is One Religion, which is obligated upon all mankind, Jews call it B'nai Noah, Christians call it Natural Law, and Muslims call it the Religion of Islam. There have been numerous Shari'a (covenants), which may exist side by side. The Muslim judge, Qatada ibn al-Nu'man (d. 720) said "al-din wahid wa al-Shari'a mukhtalifah" (religion is one, shari'a is diverse).[3]

---

1 - "Neither the Jews nor the Christians will be satisfied with you [O' Muhammad] unless you follow their doctrine of religion." Q2:120.
2 - Abdullah Al Turki, Tafsir Al Tabari, (Ryadh: Dar Aalam al-Kutub, 2003) volume 2, page 484.
3 - Qatada ibn al-Nu'man, Islamic Research Magazine, General scholarly research and jurisprudence, KSA.

THE RETURN
OF ALL REFUGEES

Fourth objection: someone else might say, "But what about the Palestinians? Shouldn't Arab governments ask The State of Israel to allow the Palestinians to go back to the Holy Land in exchange for our allowing the Jews to come back to Arab land?" Of course, one could ask for anything one wants as a condition for accepting the Arab Jews back; however, one would be wiser to postpone such a condition. Why? Because the Jews, with all their weapons and military arsenal, are still fearful and feel unsafe. Someone might call that paranoia, but to the Jews in the Holy Land it is not paranoia, it is real fear. They wake up each morning with a view of Arab guns and rockets surrounding them and enemies wanting them out of the Holy Land.

Therefore, one could postpone such a request for several years after the return of the Jews to their communities and synagogues in Arab land. When the Jews feel safe, secure, and reconciled in their homes and communities in Arab Lands, one could argue that the Jewish people and the international community will invite the Holy Land Arabs of the Diaspora, who wish to go back to the Holy Land, to return home. Why? It makes good political and economic sense and helps heal the wounds inflicted on the Holy Land Arabs! Also, the Israelis need to grow their economy and to show the world that they can live up to the commandment of reciprocity in the Torah.[1] But, for now, the Jews fear being outnumbered completely by their current Holy Land Arab residents in the coming decades who would vote to treat them as second-class citizens or expel them outside the Holy Land. In effect the Zionists in the Holy Land are afraid of the Holy Land Arabs treating them the same way some Zionist settlers treat the Holy Land Arabs today. That is why it is important to heed the golden rule—Do not do unto others what you would not have them do unto you.

In short the Jews are afraid of what is commonly known in the State of Israel as "the genetic time bomb"—Arab women bearing more children than Jewish women. So one must first assure that the minority Jews in Arab Land are safe and equal citizens. This mutual trust is a real possibility and supported by the Holy Qur'an.[2] As the Dean of Religious life at Stanford University said, " . . . building trust across [religious] divides can change [for the better] the way potential leaders think, feel and lead." [3]

It is possible to think backwards in time in terms of reciprocal repatriation. It is also possible to think forwards in time in terms of open borders and EU style commonwealth. The key is finding a sufficient common regional history. Someone wrote the Turkish Islamic creationist, Adnan Oktar and said "As-salamun alaykom my Master Mohammad Adnan. Our expectation from you in this period [after the 2010 Gaza flotilla incident] is to make a fiercer statement regarding Israel, Insha'Allah." Oktar replied:

"You want a fierce statement? Let us not do that but show compassion to these people. Why don't you try this, instead? The entire world hates Jews. Do not do this; that is a sin that is a transgression. There is no need for such bitterness in one's standpoint. As Muslims, let us show compassion, let us watch over the Jews and protect them, then these people would relax. Of course their full obedience to the Shiloh-Mohammad Mahdi is a necessity. Otherwise they would be waging a war against the Torah. I mean if they do adopt an attitude against the King Messiah, Shiloh; that is the Mohammad Mahdi, then they would be adopting an attitude against the Torah. They are praying day and night saying "O Lord, send us the Messiah"; they are praying night and day saying "Moshiach, Mosciach" [4]

---

1 - Leviticus 19:34 "The foreigner residing among you must be treated as your native-born. Love them as yourself, for you were foreigners in Egypt. I am the LORD your God."
2 - "Nor can goodness and Evil be equal. Repel (Evil) with what is better: Then the person with whom you have enmity will become your friend and intimate!" Q41:34
3 - Rabbi Patricia Karlin-Neumann, Senior Associate Dean for Religious Life, Stanford University, Letter of Support sent to the International Organization for Peace, March 4, 2009.
4 - Adnan Oktar, "Highlights from Mr. Adnan Oktar's live interview on 12 September 2011", http://harunyahya.com.

Who May Finance
REPATRIATION

Fifth objection: someone else might say, "Where is the money going to come from to restore all the synagogues and communities, so that they are sound and functional for Jews to return?" The best choice would be for a joint Arab-Jewish effort to rebuild those communities and synagogues in their land.

Allah will help the Arabs because they are performing a good deed for other people. In addition, many wealthy Jews who donate generously to the building of settlements in the Israeli-occupied territories in the West Bank will probably be glad to donate to rebuild damaged Jewish synagogues and communities in Arab lands—if Arab governments let them. Arab governments would then have loyal and productive citizens for their society by offering to grant citizenship to ten Palestinians for every Jew returned to Arab lands.

Also, Arab governments may allocate part of their military spending to build communities and places of worship, which would be far less costly than buying weapons to fight the Zionist enemy.

ZIONIST
DO NOT WANT PEACE

Sixth objection: someone else might say, but the State of Israel does not want peace. The Zionists came to Palestine in order to demolish the Muslim Shrine in Jerusalem and build the Third Temple. The Jews came to destroy the religion of Islam. Well, the facts may be contrary to that claim. The State of Israel has given back land equivalent to three times its size to achieve peace with Egypt—the Sinai Peninsula. The State of Israel signed peace treaties with Egypt and Jordan and was willing to return the Golan Heights in exchange for peace with Syria. Also, the prisoner exchange history between The State of Israel and its neighbors may also refute the above claim. To illustrate this point, four examples are provided: First, in 1967, seventeen Israeli soldiers were exchanged for 4,238 Egyptian soldiers, 553 Jordanian soldiers, and 367 Syrian soldiers held captive.[1] Second, in 1983 six Israeli soldiers were exchanged for 4,765 Palestinians and Lebanese imprisoned at Ansar camp.[2] Third, in May 1985, three Israeli soldiers were released in exchange for 1,150 Palestinian prisoners and detainees in Israeli jails, during the "Jibril deal".[3] Fourth, in 2011, the Israeli soldier Gilad Shalit was exchanged for 1,027 Palestinian prisoners, including some convicted of multiple murders and carrying out terror attacks against Israeli civilians.[4] The above numbers show an average prisoner exchange rate of one to 623. On these matters, numbers speak louder than rhetoric.

As to the claim that Jews came to the Holy Land to destroy the religion of Islam by demolishing a Muslim shrine in Jerusalem and replacing it with the Third Temple, this claim can also be refuted. For, how could a religion protected by Allah, be destroyed by the demolition of a building, even if that building is the shrine in Jerusalem or the Kaaba in Mecca? The Kaaba was destroyed two times by humans and seven times by natural causes, yet Islam was not destroyed.[5] While some radical Zionists may wish for the demolition of the Muslim shrine on the Temple mount to clear way for the Third Jewish Temple, cooler heads often prevail on this issue.[6] Jews are perfectly aware that destroying the Muslim shrine in Jerusalem would ignite the wrath of Muslims around the globe. The Jews would be at war with the very people who saved the Jews from destruction by their arch enemies—the Christians. Rabbis endowed with good judgment and common sense know that challenging the Muslims on the temple mount is not in the best interest of the Jews, and they advice their followers not to challenge the Muslims on this issue. It is fair to say, however, that the Temple Mount is sufficiently large (45 acres) and there is enough room for Jews and Muslims to worship God on the Temple mount. If pious Jews so desire, pious Muslims could help them in their endeavor to build a temple to replace Herod temple in Jerusalem. If pious Muslims are involved in the planning and building of the Third Temple, the Third Temple will last for more years than if the Muslims were challenged, ridiculed and their Jerusalem shrine destroyed.

1 - Background on Israeli POWs and MIAs, The State of Israel Ministry of Foreign Affairs, Retrieved December 4, 2011.
2 - Ivan Watson (July 16, 2008). "Lebanese Celebrate Return of Five Prisoners," Retrieved Dec 14 2011.
3 - Yedioth Ahronoth, *Encyclopedia*. Retrieved Dec 27 2011.
4 - Richard Spencer, "Israel: Gilad Shalit 'joked with military doctors over health'". The *Daily Telegraph* (London: Telegraph Media Group). Retrieved October 19, 2011.
5 - Sahih Bukhari 1509; Sahih Muslim1333
6 - Lapidoth, Ruth; Ruth E Lapidoth, Moshe Hirsch (1994). *The Jerusalem Questionand Its Resolution: Selected Documents*. Jerusalem: Martinus Nijhoff. pp. 542.

ZIONIST
AGGRESSION REWARDED

Seventh objection: someone else might say, if Arab governments agree to peace with the State of Israel, Arab governments will be acknowledging defeat, rewarding aggression by Israel. Are you asking Arab governments to concede defeat to Israel? Acknowledge losing to the Zionist enemy? In all its wars, the State of Israel claims to have acted in self-defense. Israel claims that ever since the partition plan of 1947, Jews wanted a place to call home and to live in peace with their neighbors. The Jewish people look forward to trade with their neighbors far more eagerly than they do to war. Therefore, agreeing to peace, implementing Islamic moral values, resolving humanitarian crisis of the refugees and applying Qur'anic principals is a sign of courage, not of defeat.

With open peace between Arabs and Jews, Arab governments will be conceding defeat, not to Israel, but to bigotry and hate. That is the right kind of defeat to have. Even if Arabs lose this battle to the State of Israel, Arabs will be winning the moral war against stubbornness and dogmatism.

ZIONIST
MAY REFUSE REPATRAITION

Eighth objection: someone else might say, what if the Jews refuse to come back to reclaim their synagogues and their communities? First of all, since many Jews love their countries of origin, the land of their forefathers, one would doubt that as a whole the Jewish people will refuse to come back to the land of their ancestors. It is safe to say that, if the Jews are offered such opportunity and the offer is genuine, many of them would take it. Many Jews, say that, while their bodies exist outside their native country, their hearts yearn to return to the land of their forefathers in North Africa, Egypt, Mesopotamia, Levant and Yemen.

Secondly, even if the Jews do not take the Arabs offer, the Arabs would have done the right thing. The Arabs would have proved to themselves that they can face truth with confidence in God and a clear conscience. Allah will be the Arab's witness that they did what is right in the sight of Allah.

ZIONIST
AND THEIR PLOY

Ninth objection: someone else might say, "This looks like another Zionist ploy to cause Arab governments to make more concessions for which Arabs get nothing in return." One could argue here that this is not a Zionist ploy. Why? It is a well-known fact that certain Zionists would like to bring all the Jews in the world to the Holy Land. Then they want those Jews to demolish the Muslim shrine on the Temple mount. Then they want to replace the Muslim shrine with the Third Temple as described in the biblical book of Ezekiel.[1] Such event will most likely lead to conflict and bloodshed, but those Zionists are willing to take the risk. Some Zionists do not want any Jew to leave the Holy Land and return to the country he or she came from. They would like to make the Holy Land an ethnically pure area for the Jews.

The Zionists are offering plane tickets, citizenship, no-interest loans, free language classes, rental assistance or free housing, jobs, cars, child allowance, and up to US $20,000 move-in bonus to Jews so that the Jews could leave their country and come to live permanently in the Holy Land. However, if Arabs want to disappoint those types of Zionists, then Arabs should consider giving the Jews the right of return to their Arab lands. Why? Such a plan will take an arrow out of those Zionists' quiver. Some Zionists hold Arabs and Muslims in low esteem; they do not think that Arabs will ever have the moral courage to consider correcting past inequities. They think that there is no place in Muslim-Arab hearts for non-Muslims. Coming out with such a plan will show those Zionists that they were wrong in thinking about Arabs that way.

---

1 - Ezekiel chapter 40-42.

ARABS
ARE CHEATED . . . AGAIN

Tenth objection: someone else might say, "But what is in this deal for the Arabs? It looks as if Arabs are giving up something for nothing?" A lot is in this deal for Arab countries and the Arab people. With this deal Arab countries would be correcting past errors, amending past mistakes, reconciling themselves with God, redeeming their souls, healing their wounds, and liberating themselves from worshipping their Arab identity to worshipping God the Creator of all peoples and all nations, God the Companionate, the Beneficent, the Merciful.

What could happen if Arab governments were to make such an offer—to grant the Arab Jews the right of return and grant the Arab Palestinians the right of citizenship—is that Arabs would draw themselves closer to the word of Allah.

THE THIRD POINT
THE HOLY LAND

The third point to be discussed is this: What could happen if one respects the names that Allah mentions in the Holy Qur'an? What could happen if one does not change the names that Allah chose in the Qur'an? For example, Allah describes someone who is pious, prays, fasts, and gives to charity as a *believer* (Arabic: مؤمن Mo'amen). If one changed what Allah said and called that person *infidel* (Arabic: كافر Kafer), then one would be changing the word of Allah and, therefore, would not be faithful to the word of Allah.

By the same token, if Allah calls a certain location both in the Qur'an[1] and in the Torah[2] "the Holy Land"(Hebrew: ארץ הקודש ; Eretz Ha Qodesh Arabic: الأرض المقدسة Al-Ard Al-Muqaddasah), and one insists on calling it another name, such as the Land of Palestine or the Land of Israel, then one is changing the word of Allah. The question then is this: If the area between the Mediterranean Sea and the Dead Sea is called the Holy Land in the Qur'an, then why does one, who is a follower of Muhammad calls it Palestine? Where does the name Palestine come from? Is this an Arabic name? No. Is it in the Holy Qur'an? No, the word Palestine derives from a name that came from Greek or Latin, "Palestina" translated into English as "Philistine." According to Webster Third New International Dictionary, the word "philistine" as referring to a person has several derogatory meanings[3], including "one regarded as a natural or traditional enemy because [of] belonging to a despised class" and as "a crass prosaic often priggish individual guided by material rather than intellectual values." Other meanings include "ignoramus," "outsider," and "one oblivious to aesthetics." Is it now understood why the West in general and the English-speaking world in particular do not look favorably on the name "philistine"? Philistine is a derogatory or pejorative term in English, just as *Kafer* is a derogatory or pejorative term in Arabic.

---

1 - Ibidem Q5: 21 "O my people! enter the holy land which Allah has prescribed for you and turn not on your backs for then you will turn back losers."
2 - The Harper Collins Study Bible, Exodus 3:5 (New York: HarperCollins Publishers, 2006) 88.
3 - Philip Grove, Webster Third New International Dictionary, Unabridged (Sringfield, MA: Mariam-Webster Inc. Publishers, 1993) pp 1697

PALESTINE
VS. HOLY LAND

So, why does one abandon a beautiful name that Allah gave in the Holy Qur'an?[1] If Arabs truly love Allah and respect and revere Allah's word, then one should reflect such love by using the name Allah gave in the Qur'an to the land commonly called Palestine, namely, one should call that land the Holy Land, *Al-Ard Al-Muqaddasah,* just as the name of the holy city to which the Prophet Muhammad immigrated was changed from Yathrib to Medina[2] to fulfill Allah's command. One should have no doubt that Allah will be pleased if one uses the names Allah gave in the Qur'an. Now, let's look at the word Israel or B'nai Israel. That word is mentioned more than 40 times in the Holy Qur'an, and it is mentioned approximately 2,575 times in the Holy Bible.

The criteria here, however, should not be the number of times a word is mentioned but the context in which it is often mentioned. The word Philistine is associated with "uncircumcised" people (i.e., unholy or godless people), while the word Israel is associated with "circumcised" people or people of God. According to the King James Version of the Holy Bible, Israel is defined as: one who prevails with God or one who let God prevail. Israel was a name given to the Prophet Jacob at Bethel. Israel is a name that applies to the Prophet Jacob's decedents and to their kingdom. According to the KJV, Israel means the true believer is Jesus Christ as explained by the Apostle Paul. The name of Israel is, therefore, variously used to denote 1) the Prophet Jacob, 2) the literal descendents of Jacob, and 3) the true believers in Jesus Christ—according to the LDS doctrine—regardless of their lineage or geographical location.[1] This is akin to the name "Sharif" or "Hashemite" in the Muslim tradition. The name Hashemite or Sharif is variously used to denote 1) the Prophet Muhammad, 2) the literal descendents of the Prophet Muhammad through his daughter Fatima, 3) the true believers in the Prophet Muhammad, regardless of their lineage or geographical location and 4) the modern Hashemite Kingdom of Jordan.

Now, Allah has called Palestine the Holy Land for a reason. The reason is to sanctify and purify the soul and spirit of those who visit the Holy Land. Because it is called the Holy Land, the proper mechanism to handle the Arab-Israeli conflict cannot be a secular institution but must be a religious institution with credible leadership, trusted by both sides, scholars who are considered God-fearing as well as knowledgeable about all three faith traditions.[2]

One could think of the Holy Land as a hospital—a hospital for the heart—where a sick person goes to receive treatment. People flee to such a land when they have nowhere else to go—just as Muslims flee to the Holy Lands of Mecca and Medina when they feel that their spiritual life needs alignment or realignment. Pious Jews and Christians consider Jerusalem where the Bible was revealed and Hebron where the Prophets and Patriarchs are buried, the Holy Land.[3] This is akin to Mecca, where the Qur'an was revealed, and Medina, where the Prophet and the Companions (Arabic: الصحابة Sahaba) are buried—a place to sanctify oneself. However, for some people, the illness is so severe that they want to stay in the hospital forever, and they would rather die in the hospital than die anywhere else. Also, some people choose to live in the hospital because they are afraid that if they leave the hospital, they will become sick—even die or be killed, just as Muslims yearn to travel to Mecca and Medina and live there and to die there and be buried there.

---

1 - "To test my theory about calling Philistine the Holy Land among Arabs, a visit was made to the local Mosque on George Street in New Haven, CT, Masjdul Islam, where. Shaikh Imadudeen Abu Hijleh from Palestine was there. I asked him if he would mind that we call Philistine the Holy Land instead, he had some resistance first, and then he said "there is nothing wrong with using a Qur'anic name. I am only looking for justice and dignity for my family in the Holy Land and outside the Holy Land" I told him glad tiding, this will happen. Inshallah
2 - Q9:120
3 - KJV, The Holy Bible (Salt Lake City: Published by the LDS Church, 1979) p. 708.
4 - Benjamin Abrahamson, Religious Court Judge in Jerusalem, Israel, via email dated May 15, 2012.
5 - Just as Shia consider Qum in Iran and Najaf in Iraq as Holy Lands; as Hindu Indians consider Kashi Vishwanath in Benaras, UP, a Holy Land; Sikhs consider Amritsar in the Punjab Holy Land.; and Catholics consider the Vatican Holy Land. See link for more holy places around the world. http://en.wikipedia.org/wiki/List_of_religious_sites#Bah.C3.A1.27.C3.AD_Faith

Jerusalem & Mecca

Although role of Jerusalem in Islam is not as significant as Mecca, Jerusalem is the center stage for all Muslim eschatological expectation. The centrality of Jerusalem to the Messianic hope of Jews, Christians and Muslims cannot be forgotten. This is why it is worthwhile to stress that the Jewish tradition of King Messiah and Islamic traditions of Al Mahdi (pbuh) will be fulfilled by one and the same person. Many Jews however, believe that they must not jump ahead of God and the Messiah by insisting on going back to Israel—and taking it over—by force before the Messiah comes.

In March 2010, Sheikh Tantawi, the Grand Imam of Al Azhar Mosque, the largest Islamic theological Institute in the world, feeling death near, travelled to Medina, Kingdom of Saudi Arabia, where he died few days later and was buried in Maqbaratu al-Baqī' (Arabic: مقبرة البقيع *Al-Baqi' Cemetery*). Tantawi made the journey because an Islamic tradition holds that the best and purist place on earth is *Al-Baqi' Cemetery*. Likewise, some Christians and pious Jews yearn to travel to the Holy Land, some as mere religious tourists and some as pilgrims, to purify their hearts and cleanse their souls and follow in the footsteps of their Prophets Abraham, Isaac, Jacob, David and Solomon. While Jews experience physical freedom in United States, the Holy Land is the only place on earth where a Jew can have both physical and spiritual freedom. Jews and Christians have a faith tradition originating in the Holy Land; both faith traditions are part of B'nai Israel (the children of Israel). This is an important notion to understand. The Jews are B'nai Israel, and the Christians are B'nai Israel; the Holy Qur'an affirms this likeness.[1] Both faith traditions have their Holy Books (the Tanakh in Hebrew and the Gospel in Greek) revealed completely or partially in the Holy Land. Now the question is why did Allah, the creator of heaven and earth, send another message or another messenger? Why the new message is in a totally different language and tongue from the previous two messages?

---

1 - "Then a portion of the Children of Israel believed, and a portion disbelieved: But we gave power to those who believed, against their enemies, and they became the ones that prevailed." Q61:14

UNIQUENESS
OF EACH REVELATION

When it comes to the question of new revelations two reasons are often cited: Firstly, the new revelations were given because the old revelations became corrupted through distortion, misrepresentation, twist or falsification. Secondly, new revelations were given because of the natural diversity of mankind. Each nation was given a Prophet, a Book, and a Law. Allah could have created us a single Nation (Ummah) but He chose not to do so:

> "... to each among you have we prescribed a Shariah (law) and Minhaj (custom). If Allah had so willed, He could have made you a single Ummah (people), but (Allah's plan is) to test you in what Allah hath given you: so strive as in a race in all virtues. The goal of you all is to Allah; it is Allah that will show you the truth about the matters in which ye differ." [1]

> "We sent not a Law Giver, a messenger, except to teach in the language of his own people, in order to make things clear to them: and Allah is Exalted in power, full of Wisdom." [2]

> "Had Allah sent this Qur'an in a language other than Arabic, they would have said: "Why are not its verses explained in detailed Arabic?"[3]

The Prophet Muhammad echoed the same message when he said "From amongst all those nations (ummahs) you are among the ummah that has been allotted to me and from amongst all the prophets I am the prophet who hath been assigned to you."[4] The next point will attempt to answer the question of scripture.

---

1 - Ibid Maida Q5:48
2 - Ibid Ibrahim Q14.4
3 - Ibid Fussilat Q41.44
4 - Musnad Ahmed 2614

THE FOURTH POINT
THE PURPOSE OF SCRIPTURE

The fourth point to be discussed is this: What could happen if one takes the Qur'an's word for what it says? What could happen if one did not add one's attitude, disposition or inclinations to the Qur'anic text? One is referring here to the question: why did Allah send the Prophet Muhammad to the world? The Qur'an tells us that Allah had two established religions before Islam, namely Christianity and Judaism. Why was a third message introduced?

According to the Qur'an, Allah wanted to restore the religion of the patriarch Abraham (Ibrahim) to the world. So Allah sent the Prophet Muhammad (a descendent of Ibrahim through the line of Ishmael) with a message to restore the religion of Ibrahim. In this case, Allah had to reveal the restoration message in a language other than the previous two languages and to direct the new Prophet to worship Allah by facing a new direction. Why? Jews, who believed in God and certain Christian denominations, always prayed facing Jerusalem just as the early Muslims prayed facing Jerusalem, before Allah commanded the Prophet Muhammad and those who followed him to change their Qibla (destination) from Jerusalem in the Holy Land to Mecca in the Hejaz. Then Allah revealed to the Prophet Muhammad that the holy destination (the direction of prayer) was to be different from the *Ahlul Kitab's* (Jews and Christians) destination and that neither group was to follow the destination of the other group, as recorded in the Holy Qur'an,[1]

So Allah instructed the Prophet Muhammad who received a new message in a new language and proclaimed a new Qibla that is different from the Qibla of Jews and Christians. Why? Because Allah said that Jews and Christians had irreconcilable differences and that the Prophet Muhammad should not get involved, take sides or becoming entangled in arguments over those differences. Prophet Muhammad was instructed to stop trying to resolve the dispute between Christians and Jews and to leave that to Allah.[2] In addition, Allah knows that if Allah lets more than one tradition have the same Qibla, it will be a recipe for disaster. If a single site is sacred to two religions, the fight seems almost inevitable. If what two groups consider to be divine commands are radically incompatible, they are likely to collide if they share the same space.[3]

---

1 - Ibid. Q2:145. Some Jews and Christians may face Jerusalem when they worship, others may face Shechem, and yet others may face Rome. That is why the Qur'an says that "they will not follow each other Qibla." And Q2:145: "Even if you were to bring to the people of the Book [Jews and Christians] all the Signs (together), they would not follow your Qibla (destination); and you are not going to follow their Qibla (destination)."
2 - Ibid. Q6:107: "And if Allah had pleased, they [Jews and Christians] would not have worshipped others [with Allah] and We have not appointed you a keeper over them, and you are not placed in charge of them."
3 - Miroslav Volf, Allah: A Christian Response (New York: HarperCollins Publishers, 2011) page 5.

THE PURPOSE
OF THE QUR'AN

What is the purpose of the Qur'an for Jews and Christians? Allah draws the attention of the Prophet Muhammad to the most important mission of his message in the Holy Qur'an. Allah is instructing the Prophet Muhammad about two main purposes: the first purpose the Qur'an was revealed is to clear up those things about which Jews and Christians differ.[1] If one keeps that in mind, Ahlul Qur'an and Ahlul Kitab will enjoy much better relations and avoid much of the conflict and strife over the Holy Land. One might add here that the reason Muslims controlled the Holy Land of Jews and Christians for many centuries is that both of these traditions were on each other's throats' and could not agree amongst themselves. Today however, many adherents of both traditions agree that the Jews should populate the Holy Land. Muslims should be happy about that and encourage reconciliation between those seemingly incompatible traditions. Why? The Holy Qur'an commands Muslims to reconcile between people.[2]

In addition to the above purpose—to clear up those things about which Jews and Christians differ—there is a second purpose relating to Jews and Christians in the Qur'an. The second purpose is revealed in Surah number 44, verse number 15:

> "... and say (O'Muhammad): I believe in what Allah has revealed of the Book (Torah and Injil), and I am commanded to make amends between you; Allah is our

Lord and your Lord; we shall have our deeds and you shall have your deeds; There is no contention (dispute) between us and you: Allah will gather us together, and to Allah is the return." ³

In the above verse there is a clear message to the Prophet Muhammad—and to his followers—to help make amends or to reconcile between those differing groups—Jews and Christians. Furthermore, Allah is instructing him that there is no contention or dispute "between us and you" because all revelations come from the same source—Allah.

Someone else might say, but the Qur'an says that the Prophet Muhammad was sent to all mankind. One will have to agree that the Prophet Muhammad was sent to all mankind, Arabs and non-Arabs including Jews and Christians.⁴ The Qur'an tells us that every Prophet came with a general message and a specific message. The general message is meant for all mankind, and reflects the Religion of Islam (submission to one God). There is no distinction between the Prophets. The specific message is related to the Shari'a (Law) that was assigned to an Ummah (nation). The first Religion was given to Adam (pbuh), which Jews called the Religion of the Prophet Noah and Muslims call the Religion of Islam. Thus insofar as Jews view their Religion of Noah as the first religion given to man, Jews recognize that Judaism is a form of Islam with Islam being the first religion.⁵ In other words, Judaism and Islam both converge and both were the same people during the time of Noah.

However, because Jews and Christians had their own scriptures and their own Prophets, their own Shari'a, Patriarchs and Saints, and because their basic belief systems were consistent with Islam—e.g. monotheism, social justice, forgiveness—Allah said to the Prophet Muhammad that Jews and Christians have a special status within the meaning of the Ummah (Nation) of Islam. The Qur'an is clear about the role of Jews and Christians within the restored religion of the Prophet Ibrahim as revealed to the Prophet Muhammad. As long as Jews and Christians follow the morals and ethics revealed in their own books, they should be left to worship God according to their own conscience, and their assessment should be left to Allah on the Day of Judgment to evaluate.[6] Just like, Allah warns Jews and Ahlul Kitab who do not follow the morals and ethics revealed in their scriptures. Allah also has a strong admonition for Ahlul Qur'an who do not follow the morals and ethics revealed in the Holy Qur'an.[7]

---

1 - Q16:64: "(O Muhammad) we have only revealed to you the Holy Qur'an so that you may clarify to them (Jews and Christens), that about which they differ and (as) guidance and a mercy for those who believe." The word "them" in the above verse refers to "the people of the book" (Arabic: اهل الكتاب Ahlul Kitab) the Jews and the Christians.

2 - Ibid. Q4:114 "He who enjoins charity or goodness or reconciliation between people; and does this seeking Allah's pleasure, Allah will give him a mighty reward"

3 - Ibid. Q44:15: وَقُلْ آمَنتُ بِمَا أَنزَلَ اللهُ مِن كِتَابٍ وَأُمِرْتُ لِأَعْدِلَ بَيْنَكُمُ اللهُ رَبُّنَا وَرَبُّكُمْ لَنَا أَعْمَالُنَا وَلَكُمْ أَعْمَالُكُمْ لَا حُجَّةَ بَيْنَنَا وَبَيْنَكُمْ

4 - Ibid. Q34:28: "We have sent you [O Muhammad] but as a universal (Messenger) to men, giving them glad tidings, and warning them (against sin), but most men understand not"

5 - Benjamin Abrahamson, Religious Court Judge in Jerusalem, Israel, via email dated May 15, 2012.

6 - Ibid. Ibid. Q5:48 "all of you will return to Allah [on day of Judgment], and Allah will let you know those things you differ about."

7 - Q72:23: "for any that disobey Allah and His Messenger,- for them is Hell: they shall dwell therein for a long time."

WAYS
TO CLEAR CONFLICT

Therefore, the Qur'an was not revealed so that Jews would abandon their faith and abolish their prophet Moses and abrogate their book, the Torah, in order to follow The Prophet Muhammad. The Qur'an was not revealed so that Christians would abandon their faith and abolish Jesus Christ and abrogate their books, the Greek Septuagint for Protestants or the Latin Vulgate for Catholics (aka: Christian Bible), in order to follow the Prophet Muhammad. The Qur'an was revealed for two reasons: d'awa (invitation) and Dignitism.[1] "Dignitism" means to invite Jews to follow and uphold the best morals and ethics that their own tradition has to offer as delineated in their own book, the Hebrew Torah, and to invite Christians to follow and uphold the best morals and ethics their own tradition has to offer as delineated in the Christian Bible.[2]

D'awa means invitation for those Ahlul Kitab who do not follow their faith or for people who do not have any religion, such as pagans, those who are not Jews or Christians, the Prophet Muhammad was sent to invite them all to the restored religion of the Prophet Abraham—Islam. Another view is that Shari'a of Torah—the system of 613 laws—was incorrectly being required of the non-Jewish Edomites, Ammonites and Nabateans of Arabia. The Prophet Muhammad came to release them from the Shari'a (Law) of the Torah and restore the pure monotheism of the Shari'a of the Prophet Abraham (pbuh).[3]

The Qur'an says that the Prophet Muhammad was sent to offer compassion, grace and mercy to creation and not to coerce, curse or condemn creation.[4] Therefore, if Jews or Christians chose voluntarily to follow the message revealed to the Prophet Muhammad, they are welcome to do so; and they will have their reward doubled, once for following what was revealed to them, and once for following the new message revealed to the Prophet Muhammad, as indicated in the Holy Qur'an[5] Jews and Christians should not be taunted, insulted, or ridiculed because they follow a Shari'a other than the Prophet Muhammad's Shari'a or a book other than the Holy Qur'an. They should be treated with *Ihsan*, kindness, respect, and integrity. They should be inspired and encouraged to follow the best guidance they have in their own Holy Scriptures.[6]

Allah prohibited the believers against reviling, cursing, abusing, or insulting non-Muslim or their deities[7] Therefore, as Muslims, one should treat others with respect, kindness, and integrity. One should implement the recommendations made in the recent Al Azhar Document about respect of religion "full respect of divine religions . . . . [and to] protect and fully respect [all] places of worships."[8] No coercion, no insults, and no demolition of places of worship, such as the Israeli demolition of a mosque in the Negev[9] or such as the recent fatwa issued by the Saudi Grand Mufti Sheikh Abdul-Aziz Al al-Shaikh to demolish Churches in KSA.[10] It is important for Jews and Muslims to be reminded that, God is Mercy,[11] the Prophet Muhammad is Mercy,[12] and the Holy Qur'an is Mercy.[13]

We should all be reminded that there is a difference between religion and power politics. Religion: the belief in and worship of a superhuman controlling power called Allah or God. Religion is about relationship with God and kindness to neighbor. Power politics on the other hand is about action by a person or state to increase their power or influence over people.

Power politics is not concerned with God or with kindness to other human beings. Power politics is about administering resources to maximize state power. Therefore, when the state or a religious leader issues a damaging decree they are in affect practicing power politics, not religion.

---

1 - "Dignitism" is a word coined by the author of this paper to indicate that people who believe differently from each other still deserve acceptance and respect because we are all created in the image of God. Dignitism implies that there is more than one way to worship God and to be a good human being.
2 - Ibid. Q5:66: "And if they [the Jews] had kept up [the moral and ethical teachings of] the Torah and [the Christians had kept up the moral and ethical teachings of] the Gospel and that which was revealed to them from their Lord, they would certainly have eaten from above them and from beneath their feet (which means to have comfortable and fulfilling lives)"
3 - Teshuvot ha-Rambam 2, no. 293
4 - Ibid. Q21:107: "We have only sent thee (o Muhammad) as a Mercy for all humanity."
5 - Ibid. Q28:53" "They [Jews and Christians] shall be granted their reward twice, because they are steadfast and they repel evil with good and spend out of what We have given them."
6 - Ibid. Q39:23: "Allah has revealed (from time to time) the most beautiful Message in the form of Books, consistent with itself, (yet) repeating (its teaching in various aspects)."
7 - Ibid. Q6:108: "And insult not those whom they [non-Muslims] worship besides Allah, lest they insult Allah wrongfully without knowledge. Thus we have made alluring to each people their own doings; then to their Lord is their return and [their lord] shall then inform them of all that they used to do."
8 - Associated Press, "Al-Azhar sheik proposes bill of rights, aiming to balance out Islamists in Egypt constitution", The Washington Post Foreign Policy, January 10, 2012.
9 - "Israeli police demolish mosque", Algezirah, November 7, 2010.
10 - Bill Getiz, "Persecution on the Peninsula," *The Washington Free Beacon*, April 6, 2012.
11 - Q6:54 "your Lord has ordained mercy on Himself,"
12 - Q21:107 "We sent thee not, but as a Mercy for all creatures."
13 - Q64:16 "a guide and a mercy to those who believe."

THE FIFTH POINT
VIRTUE OF LEARNING AND MERCY

The fifth point I would like to make is this: What could happen if one thought of Islam as a religion of knowledge, science, and learning? What if one thought that knowledge about revelation and knowledge about creation are the most important values in the Islamic faith? As to the Qur'an being a book of knowledge and learning, all one has to do is look at the first word revealed to The Prophet Muhammad: "Read" (Arabic: اقرا Iqra).[1] God did not start God's revelation by reciting the five pillars of Islam: 1) No God but Allah, 2) worship Allah, 3) fast Ramadan, 4) give to charity, and 5) perform Hajj. Allah started the Holy Qur'an by a succinct and powerful command: "Read!" To cement such meaning, the first attribute or quality God chose to describe God's self was not as the creator of heaven and earth as the Book of Genesis has it, not as the creator of the sun and the moon, but as "He who taught with the pen" (Arabic: الذي علم بالقلم *Allazi Allama bil qalam*).[2] To affirm these two premises, Allah made a pledge in the Qur'an. What was the first pledge or vow in the Holy Qur'an? God did not make a vow or a pledge using significant signs like the sun, the moon, the stars, the day or the night, which are all mentioned as pledges later in the Holy Qur'an. The first pledge in the Holy Qur'an is. *"Inkwell. We pledge by the pen and by what man writes"*. (Arabic: ن والقلم وما يسطرون Nun. Waal qalam wa-ma yastoroon.)[3] All of the previous verses were revealed to the

Prophet Muhammad to emphasize the virtue of knowledge and learning.

Therefore, the Qur'an is a revelation that emphasizes in its debut, in its unveiling, in its beginning, the importance of knowledge and learning. When early Muslim scholars and clerics understood such Qur'anic message, the religion of Islam produced many notable and renowned scholars whose work is being studied and taught in Eastern and Western centers of learning. Such scholars include al-Khwārizmī (d. 850 AD) in algebra, al-Razi (d. 925 AD) in medicine, al-Hamadani in physics, al-Farabi in cosmology, al-Kindi (d. 873 AD) in optics, al-Ghazali (d. 1111 AD) in theology, al-Sufi (d. 986 AD) in astronomy, al-Bīrūnī (d. 1048 AD) in physics, Ibn Hayyan (d. 815 AD) in chemistry, Ibn Rushd (d. 1198 AD) in logic, Ibn Khaldun (d. 1406 AD) in economics, and countless other scholars and scientist too numerous to enumerate.[4]

However, the Qur'an draws our attention to an important attribute, quality, and value that precedes learning and knowledge the foundation on which learning and knowledge (epistemology) firmly rests. That value is *Rahma*, which is usually translated as "mercy, grace or magnanimity." To show that our religion is about mercy and compassion is easy. One could see that in no less than 400 places in the Holy Qur'an the attribute of mercy or compassion is advocated, including in Allah's own name.[5] Also, Allah describes the Prophet Muhammad also as Rahma.[6] Therefore, Allah describes Himself as Grace and Mercy, Allah describes the Prophet Muhammad as Grace and Mercy, and Allah describe the Qur'an as Grace and Mercy. To emphasize the importance of mercy and that mercy has to precede knowledge and learning, one reads in the Holy Qur'an that Allah chose that attribute to describe God's self in the first chapter revealed to the Prophet Muhammad.[7]

Also, one reads in the Holy Qur'an that the Israelite prophet Moses spoke to Allah directly and received the Torah from Allah directly. Consequently, the Prophet Moses thought of himself as a most learned person among his people or the most learned person among Allah's creation. Allah wanted to humble the Prophet Moses and to show him that among Allah's vast creation, there exist other servants of Allah who did not receive a holy book from Allah yet are much more knowledgeable than the Prophet Moses. So Allah sent one of Allah's servants to teach Moses that which the Prophet Moses did not know. That servant of Allah was truly the most learned of Allah's creations at the time. Legend has his name as "Khedr" and he possessed a virtue that made him more knowledgeable than the Prophet Moses. That virtue was *Rahma*.[8] Therefore, mercy precedes knowledge as a prerequisite for the servant of Allah and as a prerequisite for the follower of the Prophet Muhammad. Islam acknowledges the prophet Moses and all of those who follow respect and revere his message as acceptable to Allah. Islam acknowledges Jesus Christ and all of those who follow, respect, and revere his message as acceptable to Allah. Each messenger and His followers are good human beings who worship Allah according to the dictates of their own conscience. Therefore, it is possible to be a good human being and worship Allah differently from the way your neighbor worships Allah.

---

1 - Ibid. Q96:1 "Read! in the name of thy Lord Who created"
2 - Ibid. Q96:4. This Qur'anic verse is written on the Mascot of Yale University's Sterling Library, one of the oldest universities in the United States.
3 - Ibid. Q68:1
4 - Ragheb Al Sergani, "What did Muslims offer to the world?" (Cairo: Iqra for publications, 2009) 253-395
5 - "Allah has inscribed for Himself (the rule of) Rahma" Q6:54
6 - "And Allah has only sent you (O Muhammad) as a Rahma to all creation." Q96:3
7 - "Read (Proclaim)! And thy Lord is Most Bountiful (Generous, Merciful)." Q96:3
8 - "One from among Our servants whom We had granted mercy from Us and whom We had taught knowledge from Ourselves." Q18:65

The Holy Qur'an
AND THE HOLY TANAKH

Allah admonishes Muslims to apply the knowledge-seeking commandment in the Holy Qur'an.[1] Take a selected group of young Muslim scholars *(ulama)*, about a dozen from each Muslim region, who are versed in Qur'an and in *fiqh* (Islamic Jurisprudence), and teach those Muslim scholars the biblical Hebrew language and the Tanakh. Those Muslim *ulama* will learn the Tanakh, not with the intention of finding faults, flaws, and fallacies, but with the intention of mining those books for pearls of wisdom, cognitive content, accumulated knowledge and proverbs. Those *ulama* could then become the go-to *ulama* when someone has a question about Jews and Judaism. The goal of having scholars of Arabic and Hebrew reading each other text in their own tongue has been partially realized. The Talmud was recently translated to Arabic, and the Quran and Hadith books are being translated to Hebrew. On the level of scholars, it would be worthwhile that governments support scholars is making accurate and faithful representations of the literary heritage of both faith communities.

One of the challenges is that the text in the Tanakh is translated into more than 450 languages, which include many Arabic translations[2] while the Holy Qur'an, while, translated into 105 languages, none of those translations contains an official translation of the Holy Qur'an is in the language of the Tanakh—Hebrew.[3] Therefore, one of the most vital roles of those go-to ulama, mentioned above is to translate the Qur'an into the language of the Tanakh. Why? Many Hebrew scholars, like many Arabic scholars, prefer to read and comment on text published in their own language. By having both the Qur'an in Hebrew, and the Tanakh in Arabic, Arabs and Jewish scholars may be able to reach out to each other and help improve relations between both traditions.

---

1 - Ibid. Q9:122
2 - Albert C. Sundberg, Jr., "The Septuagint: The Bible of Hellenistic Judaism," *The Canon Debate: On the Origins and Formation of the Bible*, ed. LM McDonald and JA Sanders (Peabody: Hendrickson Publishers, 2002). pp. 72.
3 - Afnan Fatani, (2006). "Translation and the Qur'an," in Leaman, Oliver. The Qur'an: an encyclopedia. (Great Britain: Routeledge). pp. 657–669.

Religion
AND GOVERNMENT

Professor Eric Nelson of Harvard University makes the point that the architects of the British and later American governments patterned themselves after a deeply religious republic. Although they held to the views of the Swiss theologian Thomas Erastus (d. 1583), that punishments, religious or otherwise, should only be meted out by a civil magistrate, and only when it benefits society, they envisioned a bicameral parliamentary system where the lower house would represent the needs and desires of the general population and the upper house would represent the rights and obligations of the people to God. Together they would make laws.[1] The English jurist, John Seldon (d. 1654) deliberately patterned the House of Lords after the Jewish Sanhedrin. What this means is that in both Western and Eastern culture it has only been in relatively recently history that religious authority has not been given a voice in government. Just as taxation without representation led to revolution, so to religious conscience without representation, inevitably leads to expressions of religious fanaticism which is uncontrolled and outside the bounds of government. For example, the suppression of religious expression during the rule of Mubarak in Egypt gave rise to many extremist Islamic organizations such as Islamic Jihad and Al Qaeda headed by an Egyptian named Ayman al Zawahiri.

As to the Arab Israeli conflict it is interesting that both sides are making claims on the land based on their understanding of their respective sacred text. A Palestinian may object here and say no, while the Zionist claim is based on a literal and selective reading of the Tanakh, the Palestinian claim is based on deeds to their lands and houses in addition to text in the Holy Qur'an. Professor Sallama Shaker at Yale Divinity School is renowned for saying, "if you are making a claim, show me the text."[2] Well there is plenty of sacred text on the side of Zionists, and sacred and secular text on the side of the Palestinians, which show that God gave the land to the Children of Abraham. Both sides claim to be the rightful heirs to the promise to the Patriarch Abraham. However, both Hebrew and Arabic religious text say that land belong to God.[3]

God appoints certain people who are close to God as guardians of the land for a prescribed period of time.[4] Religious leaders are silent about that text and politicians do not base their politics on such text. That is why all political solutions to the conflict over the last 70 years have failed, and will continue to fail until a religious solution is found based on religious text. The next point explore mutual cooperation through the concept of dignitism.

---

1 - *The Hebrew Republic: Jewish Sources and the Transformation of European Political Thought* (Harvard/Belknap, Hardcover 2010; Paper 2011).
2 - Sallama Shaker, "Religion, Globalization and the Arab Awakening of 2011," Yale Divinity School, class discussion, January 31, 2012.
3 - "The earth belong to Allah's, Allah gives the earth as a heritage to Allah's servants as Allah pleaseth" Q7:128
4 - "Allah has promised, to those among you who believe and work righteous deeds, that Allah will, of a surety, grant them in the land, inheritance (of power), as Allah granted it to those before them" Q24:55

THE SIXTH POINT
VIRTUE OF DIGNITISM AND PEACE

The sixth point is this: What could happen if one thought that there is more than one way to worship God and be a good human being? One may call such belief "dignitism." What could happen if one considers that the Prophet Moses received from Allah on Mt. Sinai a superior way for human beings to worship Allah and live their lives as recorded in the Hebrew Torah, and recognized that the Torah also says that in Allah's vast universe there are other people who worship Allah who are equally acceptable to Allah?[1] What could happen if one considers that Jesus Christ received from Allah on Mt. Carmel a superior way for human beings to live their lives and worship Allah as recorded in the Greek Gospel and recognized that the Greek Gospel also says that in Allah's vast universe there are other people who worship Allah who are equally acceptable to Allah?[2] What could happen if one considers that the Prophet Muhammad received from Allah on Mt. Hira'a[3] a superior way for human beings to live their lives and worship Allah, and recognized that the Arabic Qur'an also says that in Allah's vast universe there are other people who worship Allah who are equally acceptable to Allah?[4] What could happen if one believes that people who sincerely follow Moses, Jesus Christ, or Muhammad are equally acceptable by Allah? What could happen if religious leaders set aside the idea of supersession (one religion negating all other religions)? What could happen if religious leaders believe with certainty, when Allah said that he intentionally sent different prophets (in different tongues) to different people to test all of us?[1] What could happen if one believed in dignitism?

What could happen if one thought that Christians believe in the unity of God just as Muslims and Jews believe in the unity of God? What could happen if one thought that pious Jews and Christians believe in angels just as Muslims believe in angels? What could happen if one thought that pious Jews believe that the Hebrew Torah is the word of God just as Muslims believe that the Qur'an is the word of God? What could happen if one thought that Christians believe that the Greek Gospel is the word of God just as Muslims believe that the Arabic Qur'an is the word of God? What could happen if one thought that pious Jews love and revere their Prophet Moses just as Muslims love and revere the Prophet Muhammad? What could happen if one thought that Christians love and revere Jesus Christ just as Muslims love and revere the Prophet Muhammad? Can religious leaders then have a place in their hearts for each other? Can religious leaders truly ponder and apply the verse in the Holy Qur'an that Allah sent different guides to different people?[2]

What could happen if Muslims believed that there is more than one way to Allah? Allah said in the Qur'an that there are many ways to Allah[3] Therefore, one should be thankful to Allah for all his blessings, including the blessing of creating people of other faith traditions, including Jews, Christians, Buddhists, Hindus, and others. According to the Prophet Muhammad, a Muslim's paradise is beneath the feet of non-Muslims including Christians and Jews.[4] One's faith in Islam is not really tested until one has a Jewish neighbor on one side and a Christian neighbor on the other side, and one is kind and respectful to both of them. Some Christian and Jewish neighbors may actually be moved by such gestures; they may start investigating Islam or even embrace Islam.

The "once-in-a-millennium scholar"[1], Rabbi Adin Steinsaltz in his "The Irrelevance of Toleration" argues that finding a common foundation (Religion), and allowing for diversity was a better solution than toleration, which implies withholding condemnation for doing something wrong. That is dignitism.

---

1 - *The Harper Collins Study Bible*, Ecclesiastes 3:11 (New York: HarperCollins Publishers, 2006) p. 895.
2 - Ibid., Romans 1:20, p. 1912.
3 - Ghar Hira'a (غار راء) or Mount Hiraa is a place near present day Mecca, KSA.
4 - "We did aforetime send apostles before thee: of them there are some whose story We have related to thee, and some whose story We have not related to thee." Q40:78
5 - "To each among you (Jews Christians and Muslims) we have prescribed a law and an open way. If Allah had so willed, Allah would have made you [Jews, Christians and Muslims] a single people, but Allah's plan is to test you in what Allah has given you: so strive as in a race for all virtues." Q5:48
6 - "We sent you [O Mohammed] only as a harbinger, and to every people [such as Jews and Christians] we have sent a guide." Q13:7
7 - "Wherewith Allah guides all who seek His good pleasure to ways of peace and safety, and leads them out of darkness, by His will, unto the light." Ibid. Q5:16.
8 - "If a human being is guided to the path of Allah because of your efforts, you will be rewarded with paradise" *Sahih Muslim Book* (Cairo: Hadith Publications, 2009) Hadith number 2406 - paraphrased.
9 - Richard N. Ostling (18 January 1988). "Giving The Talmud to the Jews". *Time Magazine*. Retrieved 23 April 2010.

TOLERANCE
AND RESPECT

The peace promulgated in this paper is not the peace of one religion dominating over all other religions, Jonathan Sakes describes this concept "Our faith speaks of peace; our holy texts praises peace; therefore, if only the world shared our faith and our text there would be peace."[1] The peace one is promoting here is a peace based on dignitism, a peace based on respecting other people of faith and holding them accountable—through their own Imam, Rabbi or Bishop—to the best their own tradition has to offer.[2] Therefore, a non-Muslim neighbor should read and contemplate a summary of the morals and ethics revealed in the Qur'an, not with the intention of finding faults, fallacies, and contradictions but with the intention of finding pearls of wisdom and ethical values to understand their Muslim neighbors. By the same token, a Muslim neighbor should read a summary of the Bible ethics, not with the intention of finding faults, contradictions, and controversies but with the intention of finding pearls of wisdom and ethical values to understand their Christian and Jewish neighbors. This way the world will be a much safer and better place to live.

The Muslim's duty is to strive for all virtues according to the Islamic faith tradition and to help others to strive for all virtues according to their own faith traditions. The Muslim who truly understands the teachings of his religion is gentle, friendly and likeable. Honesty and earning trust of one's neighbor is one of the most important duties of a Muslim.³ Because Allah created all people and all traditions; and Allah asked the believer to respect Allah's decision to create many nations, peoples, and tongues when He said in the Holy Qur'an, "We have honored the offspring of Adam." Allah did not say, "We have honored only the faithful offspring of Adam"⁴ Allah honored the offspring of Adam without specifying color, creed, religion, or race. Because Allah honored the offspring of Adam, all humans are commanded to do the same: Honor all the offspring of Adam. The only criteria Allah set for such honor is "so strive as in a race in all virtues." Strive for all virtues, such as forgiveness, humility, prudence, courage, justice, temperance, chastity, charity and patience.

Therefore, if the followers of other traditions are also "striving for all virtues", the best way they know how, and Muslim religious leaders oppose them, then Muslim religious leaders are protesting Allah's plan. The role of Muslims is to "strive as in a race in all virtues" and help others "strive as in a race in all virtues."⁵ This is true Islam as revealed by archangel Gabriel to the Prophet Muhammad and his companions; and this is true Islam as believed by the early Muslims who embraced Islam when Islam spread from Arabia, thousands of miles to the east, to India and thousands of miles to the west to Spain, all within less than a century of the death of the modern times founder of Islam—the Prophet Muhammad. If religious leaders want Allah and Allah's messengers to be pleased with them "strive as in a race in all virtues." And help others do the same according to their own tradition.

The overarching theme in the Holy Qur'an is "strive as for a race for all virtues" or "strive for all virtues." The object here is not which of Allah's laws or religions one follow; rather the object here is to use such law, whether it is in Hebrew, Greek, Latin or Arabic as our basis to "strive for all virtues." The amazing news about the Holy Qur'an is that it mentions the people of the Book (Jews and Christians) using direct or indirect reference in 4,155 verses out of 6,233 verses in the Holy Quran. That is an astounding 67% of the Holy Qur'an that invites the believer to reflect and ponder on verses that relate directly or indirectly to the people of the Book (Jews and Christians).[6] What could happen if religious leaders exegete the verses in the Qur'an that sum up the meaning discussed here as a basis for Muslims relationship with Jews and Christians? Allah said in the Holy Qur'an that he created all of us to get to know each other, to get to honor and respect each other.[7]

The concept of dignitism discussed earlier is best described by Jonathan Sacks, in his book *The Dignity of Difference: How to avoid the clash of civilizations*. In it, he describes what I referred to earlier as "dignitism" as "a way of locating the celebration on diversity at the very heart of the monotheistic imagination."[8] Dignitism does not mean anything and everything goes, and it does not mean that religious leaders compromise their own faith to accommodate the way someone else believes. The concept of dignitism is that when a group shows more sincerity and adherence in interpreting and applying the word of God, God will choose that group to lead and rule. The group that strives the most as in a race for all virtues God will choose to rule and everyone should be joyous for the choice God makes. The idea of "ruling" may be relative to a specific talent or attribute.[9] "Ruling" implies measuring. Thus God could measure us and we could measure ourselves as compared to virtuous people, who "rule" society by virtue and moral values, not by their political position among us. These are the true leaders no matter what job they have in life.

Ruling does not require imposition of power on others by coercion. Allah does not impose Allah's rule over people "It is Allah who created you and some are unbelievers, and some that are believers"[10] Allah leaves it to us humans to select those among us who are fit and qualified to rule. There is a political system that God has made perfect for human use that holds moral values that are common to all traditions.[11] However, we can observe from history that any lasting political system has to include a way of changing leadership when the leaders are not acting in the best interest of their constituents. This is the best way to avoid the tyranny of dictators who use the people's money to pay for a military police to oppress their own people. This of course is the name of the game in tyrannical regimes. And, the problem with placing "virtuous" leaders in charge of the guns and money is that they can easily be turned from virtue, or give power at their death to less virtuous souls. As the Lord Edward Acton (d. 1908) said: power corrupts and absolute power corrupts absolutely, therefore, there has to be checks and balances.

Just as in an Olympic race when the competitor who invests the most time, effort, and sweat in training, preparing for, and focusing wins the competition. When the winner receives a gold medal, everyone cheers and all are happy for him or her. After all, on the Day of Judgment, all humans will be judged regarding the time they could have been happy and joyful. And yet they wasted time in conflicts and contempt.

The Italian Rabbi Elijah Benamozegh (d. 1900) develops the concept of "multi-covenant" which is similar to the concept of dignitism, discussed above. He explains that it is like groups of craftsman who gather to build a great Palace for a king. Each group thinks that it is the best and most correct, and it is indeed so, because each group is the best and most perfect in its trade. The carpenters are best at what they do.

The bricklayers are the best at what they do. The electricians are the best at what they do. What one group teaches as the best way for it to contribute to the building the Palace, would not be correct for another group. Mixing of talents and techniques between the groups would reduce the specialty and diversity needed to create the most perfect palace. The skill set, clothing and training of each group must necessarily be different. The goal of all of them is the same, and they should strive as if in a race.[12]

---

1 - Jonathan Sacks, *The Dignity of Difference* (London: Continuum Publishing, 2002) p. 9
2 - "But if they incline to peace, you incline to peace, and trust in Allah. Verily, Allah is the All-Hearer, the All-Knower." Q8:61
3 - The Prophet Muhammad reported to have said: "Shall I not tell you who among you is most beloved to me and will be closest to me on the Day of Resurrection?" He repeated it two or three times... He said, "Those of you who are the best in manners and character." (Ahmad; sahih)
4 - Ibid. Q17:70
5 - The Prophet Muhammad (pbuh) said: "My position, in relation to the prophets who came before me, can be explained in the following example: A man erected a building and adorned his edifice with great beauty, but he left an empty niche in the corner [without plaster], where just one brick was missing. People looked around the building and marveled at its beauty, but wondered why a brick was missing from that niche! I am like unto that one missing brick and I am the last in line of the prophets." (Reported by Bukhari and Muslim.)
6 - Ibn Rushd Institute, Independent Research Project, *Ahlul Kitab in the Holy Qur'an*.
7- "O mankind! We created you from a single (pair) of a male and a female, and made you into nations and tribes, that ye may know "lita'arafu" each other, [not that ye may despise each other]. Verily the most honored of you in the sight of Allah is the person who is the most virtuous of you. And Allah has full knowledge and is well acquainted with all things." Q49:13. It is interesting that "lita'arafu" has the connotation of to acknowledge and recognize, and is related to the root "bil-ma'rufi" which means to be fair, honorable, respectable and in kind man.
8 - Jonathan Sacks, The Dignity of Difference (London: Continuum Publishing, 2002) p. xi.
9 - "Those who believe, those who are Jews, and the Christians and Sabaeans, all who believe in Allah SWT and the Last Day and act rightly, will have their reward with their Lord. They will feel no fear and will know no sorrow." (Surat Al-Baqara 62)
10 - "It is He Who has created you; and of you are some that are Unbelievers, and some that are Believers: and Allah sees well all that ye do." Q64:
11 - "So judge between them by what Allah hath revealed" Q5:48
12 - Benjamin Abrahamson, Religious Court Judge in Jerusalem, Israel, via email dated May 15, 2012.

THE KEYS
OF THE HOLY SEPULCHER

It might surprise you that the physical keys to one of the most sacred Christian sites, the Christian Church of the Holy Sepulcher, have been entrusted to a Jerusalem Muslim family, the family of Nusaybah.[1] This family has held the keys to the most sacred Christian site for hundreds of years. Also, Many Jewish families who lived in Jerusalem before 1948 used to leave their children with Arab Muslim families on Yom Kippur and go to the synagogue to worship.[2] Both, the Torah and the Qur'an say that all land belongs to God.[3] God is the true owner of the land. God alone grants permission for possession of the land to certain people for a certain duration. God alone grants the land to whomever God is pleased with. Therefore, the promise for ruling the land is acknowledged in the Qur'an and the conditions by which such ruling can take place is also outlined in the Holy Qur'an. It is appropriate here to conclude with a verse in the Holy Qur'an that seeks common ground all faith traditions and seeks unity among believers:

> *"And hold fast, all of you together, to the Rope of Allah, and be not divided among yourselves, and remember Allah's favor on you, for you were enemies one to another but Allah joined your hearts together, so that, by Allah's grace, you became brethren; and ye were on the brink of the pit of fire, and Allah saved you from it. Thus Allah makes Allah's signs clear to you, that you may be guided."* [4]

In rabbinic literature it is taught that the strongest rope is a cord made up of three strands. It is my prayer to Allah SWT that the cords of Islam, Christianity and Judaism may be bound together. May religious leaders hold fast to the Rope of Allah SWT and not be divided among themselves.[5]

---

1 - Michael R. Fischbach, "Nuseibeh Family." In *Encyclopedia of the Palestinians*, ed. Philip Mattar, New York: Facts on File, 2000.
2 - Yakov M. Rabkin, *A Threat from Within: A Century of Jewish Opposition to Zionism*. (Zed Books/Palgrave Macmillan, 2006) 34.
3 - Q7:128: "Musa said to the Israelites: Ask help from Allah and be patient; surely the land belong to Allah; He causes such of His servants to inherit the land as He pleases, and the end is for those who guard (against evil)."
4 - (Surat Al Imran 3,103)
5 - Benjamin Abrahamson, Religious Court Judge in Jerusalem, Israel, via email dated May 15, 2012.

ABRAHAMIC
TRADITIONS ARE HELPFUL RIVALS

There is a place under the sun for the Abrahamic religious traditions—Ahlul Qur'an (Muslims) and Ahlul Kitab (Christians and Jews)—to interact respectfully and prosper together. Members of these traditions, inspired by their leading voices, have a clear choice before them. They can either contemptuously avoid interaction or respectfully embrace trustworthy relationships. One choice leads to suspicion, anger and violence; the other to honesty, good will and peace. What message, then, do leaders of these communities need clearly send?

The answer is simple: They need to tell their people that all members of the Abrahamic traditions were called by God to be righteous rivals—to compete with each other in greater deeds of virtue. They need each other as helpful rivals that prod each other out of complacence in doing good. But this rivalry to remain healthy must be accompanied by the divine virtue of patience. God is patient with the whole world until the final day. Humans need to follow this example.

This righteous rivalry is complicated, however, because the religious truth claims of each of the traditions tend to contradict each other in important ways that cannot be denied or compromised. Thus members of each tradition— sincerely and not arrogantly—assert the superiority of their religious doctrines and practices. They believe God wants them to courageously proclaim the truth, and they worry that the critical contest between them over salvatory truth might be superseded by their collaborative contest to surpass each other in worldly good works. To overcome this concern, the message of rival religious leaders needs to include a call to both *honestly* and *patiently* proclaim their true doctrines.

Practically speaking, the honest and patient interaction of rival traditions can produce great religious as well as social benefits. The religious benefit is the test and certification of *faith* and *patience* under the challenge of criticism. This is exquisitely provided when we interact with neighbors that call our faith and patience into question. Thus a Muslim's faith and patience is tried by a neighboring Jew who does not honor Jesus or Mohammed, or a Christian who worships Jesus and Mary as divine beings. Will the Muslim choose to treat both of them with beautiful perfection *(Ihsan)*? Likewise a Christian's faith and patience is not proven until a Christian interacts with critical neighbors: a Jew who rejects Jesus' divinity or a Muslim who calls Jesus and Mary mere human beings. Will the Christian treat both of them with the beautiful perfection of charity? And a modern Jew's faith and patience is not well proved until he or she has Christian neighbors that preach openly that Jesus is the Son of God, or Muslim neighbors who believe that taxing non-Muslims in lieu of military service *(Jizya)* is divinely commanded in Muslim countries.

God has created the world to provide humans the beneficial test of faith and patience. All should be grateful to God for making it such a wonderful and diverse world that includes religious rivals. Each ummah, people or nation was given a Prophet, a Book, and a Law. In this very remarkable Muslim scripture God reveals that He could have created us a single people or nation but—for good reason—He chose not to do so:

"... to each among you have we prescribed a Shariah (law) and Minhaj (custom). If Allah had so willed, He could have made you a single Ummah (people), but (Allah's plan is) to test you in what Allah hath given you: so strive as in a race in all virtues. The goal of you all is to Allah; it is Allah that will show you the truth about the matters in which ye differ."

Quran 5:48.

Conclusion

Religious moral values (in the Bible and the Qur'an) are the key to a comprehensive and just solution to the Arab-Israeli conflict. Just as Islamic values helped remove corruption in many countries in the Middle East, Islamic values can also be used to peacefully solve the conflict in the Middle East. By emphasizing Islamic moral values, Arab governments will be willing to allow the return of the Oppressed (Arab Palestinians) and the Scattered (Arab Jews) to the land that belonged to them— that is, dignity to the Arab Palestinians and security to the Arab Jews. By stressing Islamic moral values Arabs will focus more on what God emphasized as a priority when God revealed God's message to The Prophet Muhammad, namely knowledge, mercy, and learning; once Arab governments allow people to worship Allah according to the dictates of their own conscience, then, God will be on the side of the Arabs. With God is on Arab side, God will put in the heart of whoever is guarding the Holy Land to allow the Arabs, followers of the Prophet Muhammad, to share in the guarding of the Holy Land. This has happened before in history and could happen again in our lifetime.

It all depends on our vision for the future. It all depends on how religious leaders view our common shared history from a perspective of our common Deen (religion), and envision our future as a reconstruction of those times when religious leaders got along. The Psalter teaches "O Israel, trust thou in the LORD: He is their help and their shield. O house of Aaron, trust in the LORD: He is their help and their shield. You that fear the LORD, trust in the LORD: He is their help and their shield."[1] Rabbinic commentary says that Jethro (Prophet Shuayb) was a "B'nai Noah" (righteous non-Jew). The "Children of Jethro" were "God fearers" also called "Kenites". Targum Onkelos, the official Aramaic translation of the Torah, always translates "Kenites " as Salamai or Muslamai. In this verse there are three circles. The Children of Aaron (the priesthood), the Children of Israel and the God-fearers / Muslamai In King David's time the Children of Israel, the proto-Muslims and the proto-Christians all worshiped the LORD together.[2]

---

1 - Psalm 115:9 -12
2 - Benjamin Abrahamson, Religious Court Judge in Jerusalem, Israel, via email dated May 15, 2012.

Summary Points
TO SOLVE THE CONFLICT

The author prefers a one state solution for Arabs and Jews in the Holy Land, However, in case a two state solution is the only viable option to peace then one ought to consider the following proposal.

In exchange for the international community financing a rail road connecting Casablanca to Calcutta through Cairo, and connecting Copenhagen to Cape town through Cairo, the following points could serve as basis for such solution.

- Acknowledge the common heritage and unity by referring to Jews, Christians and Muslims as members of the same Abrahamic religion who worship God with different covenants, tongues and customs.

- Confirm the fact that the conflict is part nationalistic and part religious. The conflict is not Islam against the West—the conflict is a complex matter among local peoples who hold ethnic and religious biases. The conflict is not colonial powers against indigenous peoples. It is a local dispute. The conflict is neither secular vs. religious nor inter-religious.

- A religious dispute is easier to resolve through the concept of shared moral values and dignitism. Once the religious dispute is solved, all other aspects of the conflict will be much easier to solve.

- View all people of the region as Ahlul Kitab, people of the book. The Jews have their book, the Christians have their book and the Muslims have their book. One could find harmony between those books bases on our discussions in this book.
- View all people of the region as potential submitters (Muslims) who might submit to God under different covenants.
- Emphasize the fact that Deen (religion) is one and Shari'a (covenant) is many. The Deen is Islam and the Jews have their covenants with God, the Christians have their covenants with God and the Muslims have their covenants with God.

Repartition the Holy Land as follows:

- A Jewish majority state from the Lebanese border in the north to Beersheba in the south; From the Jordan River in the east to the Mediterranean Sea in the west. The state will be called by most Muslims in the world the Northern State of the Holy Land. The state will be majority Jewish. It may be called the Northern State of Israel by the Jews as long as they are the majority. There is precedent for people calling the same place by different names. For example: Egypt is called Misr by Arabs and Egypt by the West.
- The Arabs will have their contiguous state from Gaza and Beersheba in the north to Eilat in the south; From the Jordan international border in the east to the Egyptian border in the west; it will be called the Southern State of the Holy Land. The state will be majority Arabs with a minority Jewish population. The state might be called the Southern State of Israel by the Jews around the world. The state will be

majority Arabs. It may be called the Southern State of Palestine by the Arabs as long as they are the majority.

- The Southern State of the Holy Land will serve people and traffic moving between the African continent and the Asian continent; that is an important gateway with huge economic, social and political benefits.
- The residences of the Northern State of the Holy Land and the Southern State of the Holy Land will have the right to choose another name for their country by a majority vote of the people.
- Defuse the tension caused by the Palestinian refugee problem and the "right of return" by granting all Palestinians citizenships in the countries where they were born or currently reside.
- For the small minority of Palestinians who do not wish to be naturalized in their country of birth or residency they would be offered the citizenship of the Northern State of the Holy Land or the Southern State of the Holy Land.
- Unite Jerusalem under the sovereignty of the Northern State of the Holy Land.
- The old city part of Jerusalem to be an International "open city" accessible to visitors from all three faith traditions.

The Arab League to enact the following resolutions

- Acknowledge the new partition plan of historical Palestine.
- Calling the two new states created: the Northern State of the Holy Land and the Southern State of the Holy Land, unless they decide to call it something else on their own maps.

- Encourage member states to enact legislations calling for the return of Arab Jews to their communities and their synagogues in the MENA area with full protection for their person and their possession.
- The newly created Southern State of the Holy Land to be provided with water and electrical energy by Egypt and new housing by KSA.
- Consider all 120 settlements in the West Bank as legal and part of the Northern State of the Holy Land.
- The Arabs who currently live in the West bank would become citizens of the Northern State of the Holy Land or move to any Arab country or become citizens of the South State of the Holy Land ("SSHL").
- The State of Israel to dismantle the Separation Wall, remove the roadblocks and check points from the West Bank and call itself, the Northern State of the Holy Land.

With the above plan in place, much anticipated peace and prosperity could reign in the Holy Land and beyond. US citizens would be safe travelling in many parts of the Middle East.

Muslim jihadi groups would be busy building roads and infrastructures, tying the NSHL and the SSHL to the rest of Asia and Africa.

THE **STRUGGLE** FOR THE HOLY LAND

Epilogue

The Holy Qur'an calls on all mankind to strive as in a race for all virtues. The call to "strive" is not limited to Muslims and *Ahlul Kitab* (Jews and Christians). The call is directed towards all humanity, towards all mankind. All of us as humans are commanded to strive as in a race for all virtues.

The need to strive towards all virtue is a general commandment for all humans; it is embedded in our conscience as humans, Allah created us as nations and tribes so that those nations and tribes get to know and appreciate each other.[1] Therefore, all of us, all brothers and sisters, living on this spaceship called Earth, are commanded by Allah and rewarded by Allah to "strive".

Whether one is Hindu, Buddhist, Taoist, Confucian, Christian, Jew or Muslim, one should be looking to one's own traditions to draw the best morals and ethical values, then strive towards such values and help others to strive towards their own good morals, ethics, virtues, traditions, and values. Allah said in the Holy Qur'an that Allah sent a guide (a messenger) to every people, tribe and nation on earth in their own tongue to teach them about their own tradition, virtues and qualities.[2]

Allah is generous and just, he sent guides in the form of messengers and prophets to the four corners of the globe to teach their own people in their own tongue about Allah. Muslims have the measuring tape, the Holy Qur'an that will protect Muslims and all of humanity from going astray.

Therefore, one should not be worried or apprehensive of having non-Muslims live next door; on the contrary, one should welcome such arrangement because this is all part of Allah's plan for the universe.

---

1 - "O mankind! We created you from a single (pair) of a male and a female, and made you into nations and tribes, that ye may know each other (not that ye may despise (each other). Verily the most honored of you in the sight of Allah is (he who is) the most virtuous of you."
2 - "and to every people we sent a messenger (a guide)." Ibidem 13:7

Exhibits

THE **STRUGGLE** FOR THE HOLY LAND

Exhibit One

FREQUENCY ATTESTING TO
PALESTINE, ISRAEL & JERUSALEM
IN
THE KING JAMES BIBLE

OLD TESTAMENT

#	Book name Hebrew	Book name Greek	Book name English	Book name Arabic	Number of chapters	Number of verses
1.	בראשית	Γένεσις Génesis	Genesis	التكوين	50	1533
2.	שמות	Ἔξοδος Éxodos	Exodus	الخروج	40	1213
3.	ויקרא	Λευϊτικόν Leuitikón	Leviticus	اللاويين	27	859
4.	במדבר	Ἀριθμοί Arithmoí	Numbers	العدد	36	1288
5.	דברים	Δευτερονόμιον Deuteronómion	Deuteronomy	التثنية	34	959
6.	יהושע	Ἰησοῦς Ναυῆ Iêsous Nauê	Joshua	يشوع	24	658
7.	שופטים	Κριταί Kritaí	Judges	القضاة	21	618
8.	רות	Ῥούθ Roúth	Ruth	راعوث	4	85
9.	שמואל (א)	Βασιλειῶν Α΄ I Reigns	1 Samuel	صموائيل الأول	31	810

10.	שמואל (ב)	Βασιλειῶν Β' II Reigns	2 Samuel	صموئيل الثاني	24	695
11.	מלכים (א)	Βασιλειῶν Γ' III Reigns	1 Kings	الملوك الأول	22	816
12.	מלכים (ב)	Βασιλειῶν Δ' IV Reigns	2 Kings	الملوك الثاني	25	719
13.	דברי הימים (א)	Παραλειπομένων Α' I Paralipomenon	1 Chronicles	أخبار الأيام الأول	29	942
14.	דברי הימים (ב)	Παραλειπομένων Β' II Paralipomenon	2 Chronicles	أخبار الأيام الثاني	36	822
15.	עזרא	Ἔσδρας Α' I Esdras	Ezra	عزرا	10	280
16.	נחמיה	Ἔσδρας Β' II Esdras	Nehemiah	نحميا	13	406
17.	אסתר	Ἐσθήρ Esther	Esther	أستير	10	167
18.	איוב	Ἰώβ Iōb	Job	أيوب	42	270
19.	תהילים	Ψαλμοί psalmoi	Psalm	المزامير	150	2461
20.	משלי	Παροιμίαι Paroimiai	Proverbs	الأمثال	31	915
21.	קהלת	Ἐκκλησιαστής Ἐκκλησιαστής	Ecclesiastes	الجامعة	12	222
22.	שיר השירים	Ἆσμα Ἀσμάτων Asma Asmaton	Song of Solomon	نشيد الإنشاد	8	117

23.	ישעה	Ἡσαΐας Hesaias	Isaiah	إشعياء	66	1292
24.	ירמיה	Ἰερεμίας Hieremias	Jeremiah	إرميا	52	1364
25.	איכה	Θρῆνοι Ἰερεμίου Thrênoi Ieremíou	Lamentations	مراثي إرميا	5	154
26.	יחזקאל	Ἰεζεκιήλ Iezekiêl	Ezekiel	حزقيال	48	1273
27.	דניאל	Δανιήλ Daniêl	Daniel	دانيال	12	357
28.	הושע	Ὡσηέ Α' I. Osëe	Hosea	هوشع	14	197
29.	יואל	Ἰωήλ Δ' IV. Ioël	Joel	يوئيل	3	73
30.	עמוס	Ἀμώς Β' II. Amōs	Amos	عاموس	9	146
31.	עבדיה	Ὀβδίου Ε' V. Obdias	Obadiah	عوبديا	1	21
32.	יונה	Ἰωνᾶς Ϛ' VI. Ionas	Jonah	يونان	4	48
33.	מיכה	Μιχαίας Γ' III. Michaias	Micah	ميخا	7	105
34.	נחום	Ναούμ Ζ' VII. Naoum	Nahum	ناحوم	3	47
35.	חבקוק	VIII. Ambakum Ἀμβακούμ Η'	Habakkuk	حبقوق	3	56
36.	צפניה	Σοφονίας Θ' IX. Sophonias	Zephaniah	صافنيا	3	53

37.	חגי	Ἀγγαῖος Ι' X. Angaios	Haggai	حجي	2	38
38.	זכריה	Ζαχαρίας ΙΑ ΧΙ. Zacharias	Zechariah	زكريا	14	211
39.	מלאכי	Ἄγγελος ΙΒ' XII. Messenger	Malachi	ملاخي	4	55
			Total (OT)		929	23145

NEW TESTAMENT

40		ΚΑΤΑ ΜΑΤΘΑΙΟΝ	Matthew	إنجيل متى	28	1071
41		ΚΑΤΑ ΜΑΡΚΟΝ	Mark	إنجيل مرقس	16	678
42		ΚΑΤΑ ΛΟΥΚΑΝ	Luke	إنجيل لوقا	24	1151
43		ΚΑΤΑ ΙΩΑΝΝΗΝ	John	إنجيل يوحنا	21	879
44		ΠΡΑΞΕΙΣ ΤΩΝ ΑΠΟΣΤΟΛΩΝ	Acts	أعمال الرسل	28	1007
45		ΠΡΟΣ ΡΩΜΑΙΟΥΣ	Romans	الرومانيين	16	433
46		ΠΡΟΣ ΚΟΡΙΝΘΙΟΥΣ Α'	1 Corinthians	الأولى إلى الكورنثيين	16	437
47		ΠΡΟΣ ΚΟΡΙΝΘΙΟΥΣ Β'	2 Corinthians	الثانية إلى الكورنثيين	13	257
48		ΠΡΟΣ ΓΑΛΑΤΑΣ	Galatians	الغلاطيين	6	149

49	ΠΡΟΣ ΕΦΕΣΙΟΥΣ	Ephesians	الإفسسيين	6	155	
50	ΠΡΟΣ ΦΙΛΙΠΠΗΣΙΟΥΣ	Philippians	الفيلبيين	4	104	
51	ΠΡΟΣ ΚΟΛΟΣΣΑΕΙΣ	Colossians	كولوسي	4	95	
52	ΠΡΟΣ ΘΕΣΣΑΛΟΝΙΚΕΙΣ Α	1 Thessalonians	الأولى إلى التسالونيكيين	5	89	
53	ΠΡΟΣ ΘΕΣΣΑΛΟΝΙΚΕΙΣ Β΄	2 Thessalonians	الثانية إلى التسالونيكيين	3	47	
54	ΠΡΟΣ ΤΙΜΟΘΕΟΝ Α΄	1 Timothy	الأولى إلى تيموثاوس	6	113	
55	ΠΡΟΣ ΤΙΜΟΘΕΟΝ Β΄	2 Timothy	الثانية إلى تيموثاوس	4	83	
56	ΠΡΟΣ ΤΙΤΟΝ	Titus	تيطس	4	46	
57	ΠΡΟΣ ΦΙΛΗΜΟΝΑ	Philemon	فيلمون	1	25	
58	ΠΡΟΣ ΕΒΡΑΙΟΥΣ	Hebrews	العبرانيين	13	303	
59	ΙΑΚΩΒΟΥ	James	رسالة يعقوب	5	108	
60	ΠΕΤΡΟΥ Α΄	1 Peter	رسالة بطرس الأولى	5	105	
61	ΠΕΤΡΟΥ Β΄	2 Peter	رسالة بطرس الثانية	3	61	
62	ΙΩΑΝΝΟΥ Α΄	1 John	رسالة يوحنا الأولى	5	105	

117

63	ΙΩΑΝΝΟΥ Β΄	2 John	رسالة يوحنا الثانية	1	13
64	ΙΩΑΝΝΟΥ Γ΄	3 John	رسالة يوحنا الثالثة	1	15
65	ΙΟΥΔΑ	Jude	رسالة يهوذا	1	25
66	ΑΠΟΚΑΛΥΨΙΣ ΙΩΑΝΝΟΥ	Revelation	سفر الرؤيا	22	404
		Total (NT)		260	7958
		Total		1189	31173

Exhibit Two

FREQUENCY ATTESTING TO PALESTINE, ISRAEL & AHLUL KITAB THE HOLY QUR'AN

Number	Anglicized name	Arabic name	English Translation	Frequency of Ahlul Kitab[1]
1	al-Fatihah	al-faatiHah	The Opening	2
2	al-Baqarah	al-baqarah	The Cow	185
3	Al-Imran	aali-`imraan	The Family Of Imran	140
4	an-Nisa'	an-nisaa'	Women	56
5	al-Ma'idah	al-maa'idah	The Food	84
6	al-An`am	al-an`aam	The Cattle	72
7	al-A`raf	al-a`raaf	The Elevated Places	175
8	al-Anfal	al-anfaal	The Spoils Of War	3
9	at-Taubah	at-tawbah	Repentance	39
10	Yunus	yoonus	Jonah	33
11	Hud	hood	Hud	77
12	Yusuf	yoosuf	Joseph	101
13	ar-Ra`d	ar-Ra`d	The Thunder	12
14	Ibrahim	ibraheem	Abraham	22
15	al-Hijr	al-Hijr	The Rock	39
16	an-Nahl	an-naHl	The Bee	33
17	bani Isra'il	banee Israa'eel	The Israelites	36
18	al-Kahf	al-kahf	The Cave	65
19	Maryam	maryam	Mary	75
20	Ta Ha	Taa haa	Ta Ha	110
21	al-Anbiya'	al-anbiyaa'	The Prophets	70
22	al-Hajj	al-Hajj	The Pilgrimage	22
23	al-Mu'minun	al-mu'minoon	The Believers	21
24	an-Nur	an-noor	The Light	2
25	al-Furqan	al-furqaan	The Criterion	8
26	ash-Shu`ara'	ash-shu`araa'	The Poets	160
27	an-Naml	an-naml	The Ant	55
28	al-Qasas	al-qasas	The Narrative	66
29	al-`Ankabut	al-`ankaboot	The Spider	23
30	ar-Rum	ar-room	The Romans	4
31	Luqman	luqmaan	Lukman	2
32	as-Sajdah	as-sajdah	The Adoration	8
333	al-Ahzab	al-aHzab	The Allies	5

---

[1] Ahlul Kitab is a term that includes Jews, Christians and Israelites.

34	Saba'	as-Saba'	Sheba	6
35	al-Fatir	al-faaTir	The Creator	15
36	Ya Sin	yaa seen	Ya Sin	20
37	as-Saffat	aS-Saaffaat	The Rangers	82
38	Sad	Saad	Sad	33
39	az-Zumar	az-zumar	The Companies	4
40	al-Mu'min	al-mu'min	The Forgiving One	39
41	Ha Mim Sajdah	haa meem sajdah	Revelations Well Expounded	2
42	ash-Shura	ash-shooraa	The Counsel	8
43	az-Zukhruf	azl-zukhruf	The Embellishment	2
44	ad-Dukhan	ad-dukhaan	The Evident Smoke	17
45	al-Jathiyah	al-jaathiyah	The Kneeling	4
46	al-Ahqaf	al-aHqaaf	The Sandhills	4
47	Muhammad	muHammad	Muhammad	2
48	al-Fath	al-fatH	The Victory	2
49	al-Hujurat	al-Hujuraat	The Chambers	0
50	Qaf	qaaf	Qaf	4
51	adh-Dhariyat	adh-dhaariyaat	The Scatterers	23
52	at-Tur	aT-Toor	The Mountain	1
53	an-Najm	an-najm	The Star	18
54	al-Qamar	al-qamar	The Moon	27
55	ar-Rahman	ar-raHmaan	The Merciful	0
56	al-Waqi`ah	al-waaqi`ah	That Which is Coming	0
57	al-Hadid	al-Hadeed	The Iron	4
58	al-Mujadilah	al-mujaadilah	She Who Pleaded	0
59	al-Hashr	al-Hashr	The Exile	8
60	al-Mumtahanah	al-mumtaHanah	She Who is Tested	6
61	as-Saff	as-saff	The Ranks	3
62	al-Jumu`ah	al-jumu`ah	The Day of Congregation	4
63	al-Munafiqun	al-munafiqoon	The Hypocrites	1
64	at-Taghabun	at-taghaabun	The Cheating	0
65	at-Talaq,	aT-Talaaq	The Divorce	0
66	at-Tahrim	at-taHreem	The Prohibition	3
67	al-Mulk	al-mulk	The Kingdom	0
68	al-Qalam	al-qalam	The Pen	20
69	al-Haqqah	al-Haaqqah	The Inevitable	3
70	al-Ma`arij	al-ma`aarij	The Ladders	0
71	Nuh	nooH	Noah	28
72	al-Jinn	al-jinn	The Jinn	0
73	al-Muzammil	al-muzammil	The Mantled One	2
74	al-Mudathir	al-muddaththir	The Clothed One	0
75	al-Qiyamah	al-qiyaamah	The Resurrection	0
76	al-Insane	al-insane	The Man	0
77	al-Mursalat	al-mursalaat	The Emissaries	0
78	an-Naba'	an-naba'	The Tidings	0
79	an-Nazi`at	an-naazi`aat	Those Who Pull Out	12
80	`Abasa	`abasa	He Frowned	0
81	at-Takwir	at-takweer	The Cessation	0
82	al-Infitar	al-infiTaar	The Cleaving Asunder	0
83	at-Tatfif	at-taTfeef	The Defrauders	0
84	al-Inshiqaq	al-inshiqaaq	The Rending	0

85	al-Buruj	al-burooj	the Constellations	11
86	at-Tariq	aT-Taariq	The Night-Comer	0
87	al-A`la	al-A`laa	The Most High	2
88	al-Ghashiya	al-ghaashiyah	The Overwhelming Calamity	0
89	al-Fajr	al-fajr	The Dawn	0
90	al-Balad	al-balad	The City	0
91	ash-Shams	ash-shams	The Sun	0
92	al-Layl	al-lail	The Night	0
93	ad-Duha	aD-DuHaa	The Early Hours	0
94	al-Inshirah	al-inshiraaH	The Expansion	0
95	at-Tin	aT-Teen	The Fig	0
96	al-`Alaq	al-`alaq	The Clot	0
97	al-qadr	al-qadr	The Majesty	0
98	al-Bayyinah	al-bayyinah	The Proof	5
99	al-Zilzal	al-Zilzaal	The Shaking	0
100	al-`Adiyat	al-`aadiyaat	The Assaulters	0
101	al-Qari`ah	al-qaari`ah	The Terrible Calamity	0
102	at-Takathur	at-takaathur	Worldly Gain	0
103	al-`Asr	al-`asr	Time	0
104	al-Humazah	al-humazah	The Slanderer	0
105	al-Fil	al-feel	The Elephant	0
106	al-Quraysh	al-quraish	The Quraish	0
107	al-Ma`un	al-maa`oon	The Daily Necessaries	0
108	al-Kauthar	al-kauthar	Abundance	0
109	al-Kafirun	al-kaafiroon	The Unbelievers	0
110	an-Nasr	an-naSr	The Help	0
111	al-Lahab	al-lahab	The Flame	0
112	al-Ikhlas	al-ikhlaaS	The Unity	0
113	al-Falaq	al-falaq	The Daybreak	0
114	an-Nas	an-naas	The Men	0

Exhibit Three

Ethnic Cleansing of Jews from the Arab World

"WHEN I SEE A JEW BEFORE ME, I KILL HIM. IF EVERY ARAB DID THIS, IT WOULD BE THE END OF THE JEWS."
- Syrian Minister of Defense Mustafa Tlass

	# of Jews in 1948	Today
Algeria	140,000	100
Egypt	75,000	100
Iraq	150,000	35
Lebanon	20,000	100
Libya	38,000	0
Morocco	265,000	5,500
Syria	30,000	100
Tunisia	105,000	1,500
Yemen	55,000	200

AN ENTIRE HISTORY ERASED
Arab Jews lived as 2nd class citizens in the Arab world for centuries until the mid 20th century, when systematic policies of ethnic cleansing began.

MASS MURDER
Massacres were carried out against Jewish communities which had existed for centuries. Arab governments terrorized Jewish communities in order to push them out of the country.

STRIPPED OF CITIZENSHIP
Jews in countries such as Libya and Syria were stripped of their citizenship for no reason, only because they were Jews. They became stateless refugees, and were forced to find a new home.

CONFISCATION OF PROPERTY
Arab governments seized homes, businesses, bank accounts, and property. When expelled, Jews were only allowed to leave with one suitcase and little or no cash. Arab Jews lost everything they had.

SYNAGOGUES DESTROYED
As a final step, Jewish places of worship were destroyed, leaving little evidence of what was once known as Arab Jewry. Today, most Arab Jews live in Israel and the United States of America.

Number of Jews in the Arab World: 878,000 (1948) → 7,635 (Today)

...and now they say the Jewish State does not have a right to exist...

When will this hatred end?

Exhibit Four

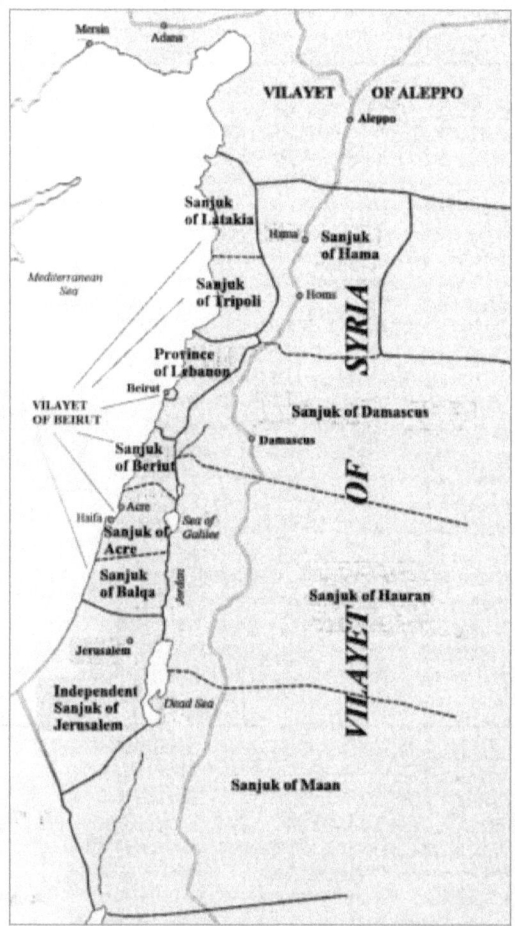

"Independent" Sanjak of Jerusalem shown within Ottoman administrative divisions in the Eastern Mediterranean coast after the reorganisation of 1887–88 AD.

source: Ottoman Syria from Wikipedia, the free encyclopedia.

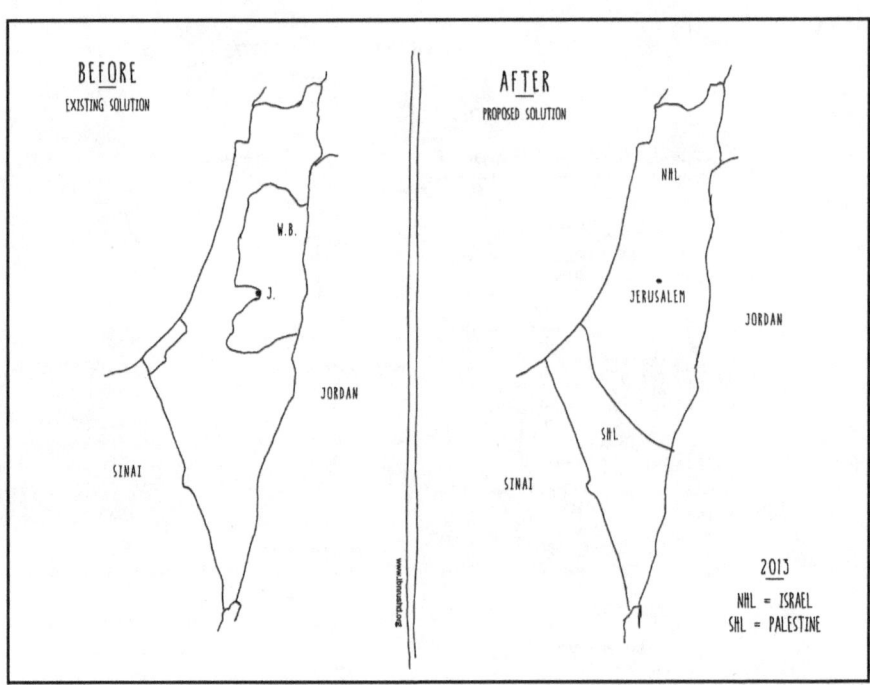

Possible land swap between
Israel and Palestine

THE **STRUGGLE** FOR THE HOLY LAND

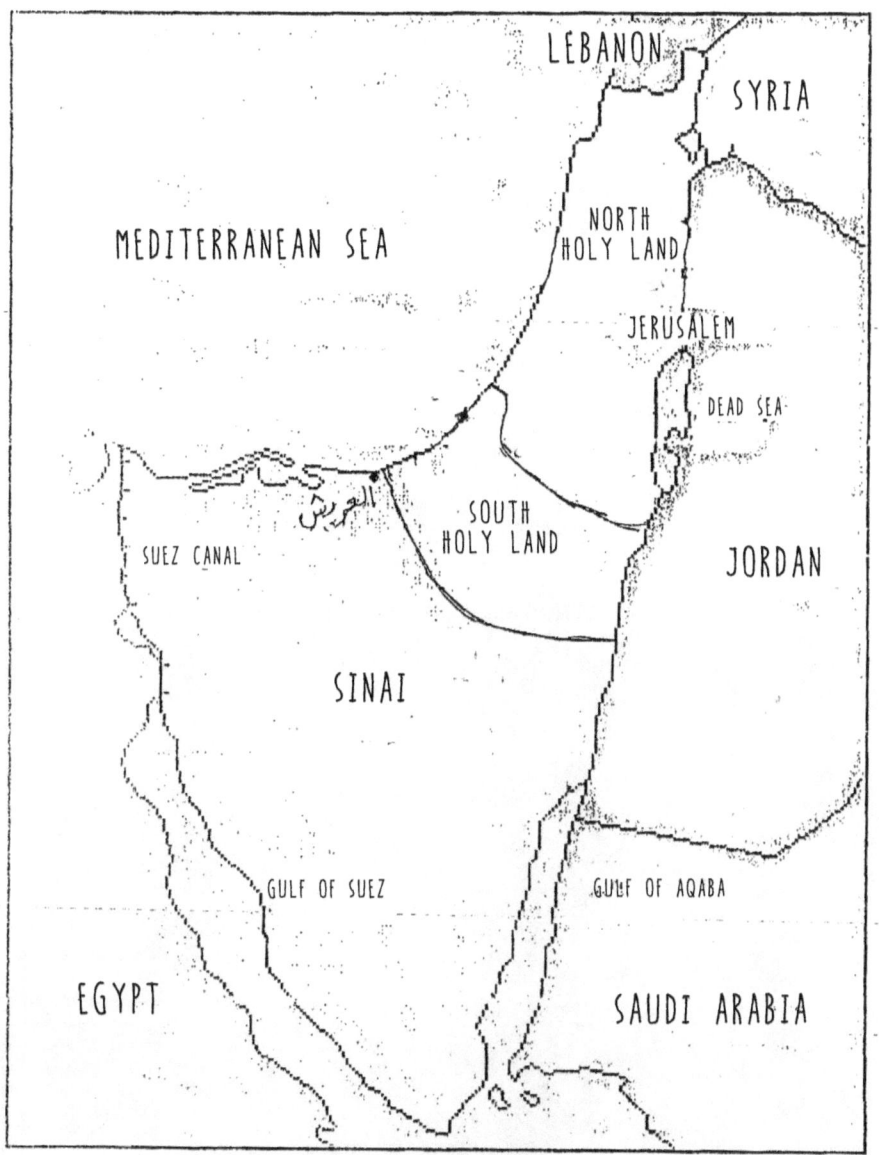

Possible land swap between
Israel, Palestine and Egypt

THE **STRUGGLE** FOR THE HOLY LAND

Bibliography

1. Rachel Scott, *The Challenge of Political Islam* , (Stanford: Stanford University Press, 2010).
2. Carl Brown, *Religion and State*, (New York: Columbia University Press, 2000)
3. John Esposito, *Makers of Contemporary Islam*, (Oxford: Oxford University Press, 2001)
4. Shireen Hunter, *Modernization, Democracy and Islam*, (Westport: Preager Publishers, 2005)
5. S. Ayse Kadayifci-Orellana, *Standing on an Isthmus*, (Plymouth: Lexington Books, 2007)
6. Ellen Lust, *The Middle East*, (Stanford: CQ Press, 2010)
7. John Esposito, *What Everyone Needs to know about Islam,* (Oxford: Oxford University Press, 2001)
8. W. Montgomery Watt, *Islamic Philosophy and Theology* , (New Jersy: Aldine Publishers, 2009)
9. Mark R. Cohen, *Under Crescent and Cross*, (Princeton: Princeton University Press, 1996)
10. Kenneth Craig, *Muhammad and the Christian*, (Oxford: One world Publication, 1999)
11. Bernard Lewis, *What Went Wrong?* , (New York: Oxford University Press, 2002)
12. Kenneth Craig, *The Call of the Minaret,* (New York: Oxford University Press, 1964)

13. Jacob Lassner, *Jews and Muslims in the Arab World,* (Maryland: Rowman and Littlefield publishers, 2007)
14. Michael Laskier and Yacoob Lev, *The Convergence of Judaism and Islam,* (Gainsville: University Press of Florida, 2011)
15. Jonathan Sacks, *The Dignity of Difference*, (London: Continuum Press, 2002)
16. Raymond Baker, *Islam Without Fear,* (Boston: Harvard Collage Press, 2003)
17. Norman Stillman, *The Jews of Arab Lands,* (Oxford: Oxford University Press, 1979)
18. David Liepert, *Muslim Christian and Jew,* (Toronto: Faith and Life Publishing, 2010)
19. Miroslav Volf, *A Public Faith,* (Grand Rapids: Brazos Press, 2011)
20. Rachel Scot, *The Challenge of Political Islam,* (Stanford: Stanford University Press, 2010)
21. Miroslav Volf, *Allah: A Christian Response,* (New York: Harper Collins Publishers, 2011)
22. Peter L. Burger, *"The Desecularization of the World"*, (Michigan: Wm. B. Eerdmans Publishing, 1999)
23. Abdullah Yûsuf Ali, *The Meaning of the Holy Qur'an,* (Maryland: Amana Publications, 2009)
24. Malka H. Schlewitz, *The Forgotten Millions: the Modern Jewish Exodus from Arab Land* (New York: Continuum, 2000).
25. James Carroll, *Constantine's Sword: The Church and the Jews* (New York, Houghton Mifflin Company, 2001)

THE **STRUGGLE** FOR THE HOLY LAND

THE **STRUGGLE** FOR THE HOLY LAND

About the Author

Omer Salem is a Senior Fellow of the Foundation of Religious Diplomacy, New York City, and is founder of the **Ibn Rushd Institute for Dialog** based in Egypt and the USA, an inter-religious research association. Salem promotes the importance of using Islamic moral values as the basis for conflict resolution. He has been invited to various churches, synagogues, mosques and international conferences, where he has spoken before audiences that included members of the U.S. Senate in Washington, D.C. and members of the Israeli Knesset in Jerusalem.

Dr. Salem is an honorary member of the Worldwide Association of al-Azhar Graduates. He is a candidate for PhD in Islamic Studies from the multi-university Graduate Theological Foundation and Al Azhar University in Cairo, he holds a Master's Degree from the Yale University Divinity School, and a Bachelor of Science Degree from the University of California at Berkeley.

Salem, an American-Sunni Muslim, was born in Egypt, establish a career in engineering, real estate and investment in California's Silicon Valley, and is a frequent preacher among the New Haven, Connecticut Muslim community. In California he assembled a group of representatives of various faith communities across the USA and the Middle East to consider options for peace in the Holy Land based on Islamic moral values. The group produced a related white paper that is the basis of the Mellata Ibrahim ("MI") Initiative that has gained support from various religious and civil society organizations and Stanford University.

Omer currently lives with his wife and four children in New Haven, Connecticut USA.

A

www.ingramcontent.com/pod-product-compliance
Lightning Source LLC
Chambersburg PA
CBHW030444300426
44112CB00009B/1152